A Wild

LIZARDS

STEPHEN SWANSON

Contents

Opposite: The Central Netted Dragon changes its colour when its body temperature changes.

Introduction

Lizards are reptiles and therefore ectothermic (cold-blooded) animals, as opposed to the endothermic (warm-blooded) mammals and birds. "Cold-blooded" is a widely used but somewhat misleading term. In reality, an active lizard's blood is no colder than that of a warm-blooded animal. The difference is that lizards use an external source, the sun (either directly or indirectly) to regulate their body temperature, whereas mammals and birds generate their body heat from within.

A lizard's skin is covered with dry scales, in contrast to the feathers of birds, hair of mammals, or the damp, naked skin of amphibians. A typical lizard is an alert, sun-loving reptile with four strong limbs, each with five toes and claws. It has blinking eyes, visible ear openings and a long tail. But there is great variation in appearance and behaviour among lizards and many do not fit this general description. In particular, some lizards have no visible limbs and in this respect resemble snakes. These snake-like lizards can be distinguished from snakes by their broad tongue. A snake's tongue is slender and forked.

Lizards have the numbers in Australia, where there are more species than all other reptiles combined. About 620 lizards in five families occur throughout the continent, with greatest concentrations in the tropical north and arid central regions. A few lizards show a remarkable degree of cold-tolerance. Tasmania's Northern Snow Skink (*Niveoscincus greeni*) lives above the treeline on Tasmania's highest peaks. It is active on the edges of mountain streams at low temperatures and hibernates each winter beneath a deep drift of snow.

Australians are generally tolerant of lizards. We don't feel threatened by them in the way some people feel threatened by snakes. In tropical Australia the Asian House Gecko (*Hemidactylus frenatus*) looks down at us from the bedroom wall and signals the setting of the sun with its "crk-crk-crk-crk-crk" call. In backyards across the sprawling suburbs of eastern Australia's largest cities, Garden Skinks (*Lampropholis guichenoti*) scamper over paths, and gardeners unearth clusters of their small white eggs in the compost heap.

Although Asian House Geckoes and Garden Skinks do very well from their association with humans, this can't be said for most other lizards. In particular, questionable land clearing practices result in widespread destruction or degradation of natural habitat and this threatens the survival of some lizards.

Opposite: An elevated stance and pale belly help an Eyrean Earless Dragon (*Tympanocryptis tetraporophora*) reflect heat from a hot rock surface.

Lizard Behaviour

Lizards are most common in hot climates because they are ectothermic (cold-blooded) and require heat from the sun to maintain an operating body temperature. Much of a lizard's day-to-day activity is linked to maintaining its body temperature at an optimum level. Diurnal lizards typically emerge from cover in the morning and bask in the sun. As they begin to overheat, they move to a shaded area, lift the body from the hot ground and may open the mouth and pant to cool down. This cycle is repeated throughout the course of the day to keep body temperature relatively stable.

Lizards need to stay warm in order to be swift enough to chase their quarry and escape from predators. Many animals prey on lizards and it is often the lizard's speed that saves it.

Nocturnal lizards like geckoes shelter from direct sunlight during the day, but warm up by keeping the body in contact with a sun-warmed surface. Within a rock crevice, a gecko might move between warm and cool places. Geckoes emerge on warm nights and maintain body temperature by lying flat against a warm rock face or foraging across a day-warmed sand plain.

Most lizards eat live food and are often stimulated into action by the movement of their prey. Insects are the main food for the majority of lizards, and these are actively chased down, or ambushed. A large monitor prefers more substantial prey and has no difficulty swallowing a fully grown rabbit. Monitors are also opportunistic feeders and will dine on the carcass of a road-killed animal or on meat scraps left behind at a barbecue in a picnic ground. A few lizards such as the ponderous Shingleback (*Tiliqua rugosa*) feed mainly on plants.

A lizard's keen eyesight is usually its primary means of finding food and avoiding predators. Some burrowing skinks have small rudimentary eyes, which suggests that vision plays a minor role in a subterranean lifestyle.

Most lizards have a visible ear opening, but in some cases it is covered by scales. Hearing is an obvious part of social interaction between vocal lizards such as geckoes.

Lizards have a well-developed sense of smell. In addition they have a Jacobson's organ, located on the roof of the mouth, which analyses (in effect, smells)

minute particles picked up by the tongue from the air or an object. This is why a lizard constantly protrudes its tongue.

Most lizards lay eggs and these are deposited by the female in a carefully constructed nesting burrow in the soil, in a tight crevice, or in loose earth beneath rocks and logs. However, some skinks — especially larger skinks and those inhabiting cool southern regions — give birth to live young.

Above: Male Yellow-spotted Monitors (*Varanus panoptes*) in combat. **Opposite, top:** Boyd's Forest Dragon (*Hypsilurus boydii*) feeds mainly on insects.

Identifying Lizards

Lizards are closely related to snakes. A snake is best described as an elongated reptile with no obvious limbs. Some legless lizards and skinks also fit this description, but neither legless lizards nor skinks have a slender forked tongue.

Australian lizards are in five families: Geckoes (Gekkonidae), legless lizards (Pygopodidae), dragons (Agamidae), monitors (Varanidae) and skinks (Scincidae).

Geckoes are small nocturnal lizards with non-overlapping scales, four well-developed limbs, a broad tongue and a fixed transparent disc covering the eye.

Legless lizards are elongated with no apparent limbs, overlapping body scales, a fixed transparent disc covering the eye and a broad tongue. They have degenerate hindlimbs that are flap-like and generally held flush against the body. Legless lizards are small to medium-sized diurnal or nocturnal lizards.

Dragons have non-overlapping scales, moveable eyelids, a broad tongue and four well-developed limbs. Many dragons have prominent spiny scales. Dragons are small to large diurnal lizards.

Monitors have non-overlapping scales, strongly developed limbs and a slender forked tongue. Conveniently, they regularly protrude their tongue as if to identify themselves. Monitors are small to very large diurnal lizards.

The greatest variation occurs within the skink family. Skinks have overlapping body scales and a broad tongue. Most have smooth scales, but some have spiny or heavily keeled scales. Skinks usually have moveable eyelids, but some have a fixed transparent disc covering the eye. Most have a normally proportioned body and four well-developed limbs, but some are elongated with degenerate limbs or no external trace of limbs. A skink's degenerate limbs are stick-like and are held out from the body. Skinks are small to large diurnal or nocturnal lizards.

Identifying lizards at the species level can be difficult because of the variability of colour and pattern within many species and a similarity in appearance of some related species. A positive identification usually requires close examination and consequent handling of the lizard, but it is unlawful to pick up a lizard in the wild without a specific permit to do so. Some small skinks cannot be identified without a detailed, often microscopic examination of their scale characters. Sometimes the characters used to separate one species from another are open to interpretation and even professional herpetologists can have difficulty separating closely related lizards. A majority of lizards can be identified, at least tentatively, by referring to a well-illustrated field guide with accompanying distribution maps.

MONITOR (Varanidae)

Above: A Perentie (*Varanus giganteus*) protrudes its snake-like tongue.

GECKO (Gekkonidae)

Above: Like all geckoes, the Smooth Knob-tailed Gecko (*Nephrurus levis*) has a fixed transparent disc covering its eye.

DRAGON (Agamidae)

Above: The Southern Forest Dragon (*Hypsilurus spinipes*) displays the spiny scales typical of many dragon lizards.

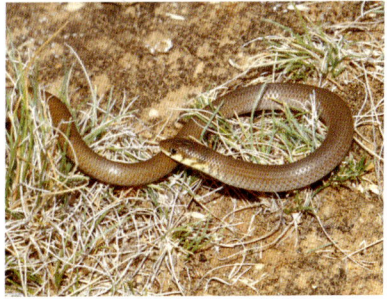

LEGLESS LIZARD (Pygopodidae)

Above: The small flap-like hindlimbs of Moller's Delma (*Delma molleri*) are usually held flush against its sides and are not immediately noticeable.

SKINK (Scincidae)

Above: An Eastern Fire-tailed Skink (*Morethia taeniopleura*) is a typical skink, with shiny overlapping scales.

SKINK (Scincidae)

Above: Some skinks like this Shark Bay Broad-blazed Slider (*Lerista varia*) have an elongate body and degenerate limbs.

Predators & Threats

For the most part, lizards sit towards the bottom of the food chain and are constantly avoiding predators. Many animals eat lizards — not least larger lizards — but also snakes, crocodiles, birds-of-prey, carnivorous marsupials, dingoes and feral animals like cats and foxes. Threats can also come from unlikely directions. In a case of insect's revenge, the insectivorous Northern Dtella (*Gehyra australis*) is occasionally seized and eaten by a large praying mantis.

Lizards are an important part of the traditional diet of Indigenous Australians. In central Australia, Aboriginal women use digging sticks to dig a Sand Monitor (*Varanus gouldii*) from its burrow. The monitor is given a blow to the head and roasted whole on a bed of hot coals.

When confronted by a predator, a lizard's first line of defence is to remain unseen and many have a colour and pattern that provide an excellent camouflage. Resting flush on a lichen-encrusted tree trunk a Southern Leaf-tailed Gecko (*Saltuarius swaini*) is easily overlooked. The Lace Monitor (*Varanus varius*) escapes by scaling the trunk of a tall tree. A Central Netted Dragon (*Ctenophorus nuchalis*) rarely strays far from its burrow and quickly disappears into it when approached. Mitchell's Water Monitor (*Varanus mitchelli*) drops into the water from an overhanging tree branch and hides under litter on the bottom of the river. If a lizard's avenue of escape is blocked, it is time for pretence. A cornered Frilled Lizard (*Chlamydosaurus kingii*) stands on its hindlimbs, extends its frill and opens its mouth to face an aggressor. It uses every trick at its disposal to look larger and more fierce than it actually is, but at the first opportunity, turns and runs on its hindlegs to the nearest tree. When a lizard realises that its cover has been blown, it takes flight; only as a last resort will it bite.

Lizards are protected by law in all Australian States. But statutory protection does not protect the many thousands that are killed annually on roads. More importantly, it does not protect the millions of lizards that are permanently removed from the Australian landscape by the wholesale clearing of their habitat. The key to ensuring the survival of Australia's lizards is to provide adequate areas of natural habitat in conservation reserves, and to control feral animals within those reserves.

Few Australian lizards are considered endangered, but the continued existence in the wild of some remnant species like the Pygmy Blue-tongue (*Tiliqua adelaidensis*) of South Australia and the Nangur Spiny Skink (*Nangura spinosa*) of south-eastern Queensland is of concern. Captive breeding programs for these and other species with small, geographically restricted populations are essential to ensure their survival in the event of a sudden decline of wild populations.

Opposite, bottom: When confronted by a predator, a Frilled Lizard (*Chlamydosaurus kingii*) opens its mouth and erects its frill to appear larger than it actually is. **Top:** The endangered Pygmy Blue-tongue (*Tiliqua adelaidensis*) occurs in a few small areas of remnant grassland near the town of Burra in South Australia. **Above:** Dingoes are one of the few natural enemies of a large Lace Monitor (*Varanus varius*).

Lizards as Pets

When children are given an opportunity to keep Australian native wildlife as pets, they are more likely to grow into adults with an understanding and appreciation of our natural heritage. Herpetoculture, or the keeping of reptiles as pets, is an increasingly popular activity in Australia and lizards make an ideal beginner reptile for a budding amateur herpetologist.

All reptiles, including lizards, are protected by law in Australia and cannot be taken from the wild. In most cases you will need to obtain a licence from the relevant State government wildlife protection authority to keep a lizard.

A lizard that occurs naturally in the region where you live will have no need for artificial heating during cold weather. In south-eastern Australia, large lizards like the Eastern Blue-tongue (*Tiliqua scincoides scincoides*), Cunningham's Skink (*Egernia cunninghami*) and Eastern Bearded Dragon (*Pogona barbata*) can be kept outside in a simple, walled enclosure all year round. The enclosure should be located in a sunny position and built of brick with an internal smooth lining to stop the lizards from climbing out. An open, circular section of corrugated water-tank steel, sunk 20 cm into the ground, is a simple alternative. Inside the enclosure raised, well-drained areas with hollow logs or other cover will ensure a dry shelter site for the residents.

A glass aquarium fitted with a lid, or a glass-fronted terrarium constructed of metal or timber, makes a suitable enclosure for smaller lizards. It is important that it has adequate ventilation and can be easily cleaned. Commercially produced terrariums, specifically designed for reptiles, are available from pet stores.

Lizards from tropical Australia or desert regions kept in southern climates need to be provided with artificial heating. Heating mats for the floor of the cage, or heating lamps which provide a basking site, can be purchased from pet stores.

Arrange the terrarium interior to match the lizard's habitat preference. Use flat rocks to form crevices for a Spiny-tailed Skink (*Egernia stokesii*), or provide a deep layer of red sand for a Broad-banded Sand Swimmer (*Eremiascincus richardsonii*).

Most lizards eat live food: worms, snails, grasshoppers and other insects can be collected from the garden. Crickets, wood roaches or mice are available from pet stores, or can be bred at home. Some captive lizards (particularly large skinks) will eat fruit, vegetables and canned pet food. A monitor's diet of live food can be supplemented with meat and eggs.

Captive lizards that are kept clean, warm and provided with fresh water and appropriate food, generally thrive. They make fascinating and engaging pets and some lizards live for many years in captivity.

Opposite, top: Lizards make fascinating pets. **Above:**
Eastern Water Dragons (*Physignathus lesueurii lesueurii*) thrive
in captivity when provided with a spacious enclosure.

Geckoes

Family: Gekkonidae

Geckoes can be found in suitable habitats worldwide, with about 110 species occurring in Australia. They are small, innocuous, nocturnal lizards. Most geckoes have a smooth, velvety skin, while others have a covering of low spiny scales, giving them a rough texture.

Most are secretive and, because they move about under cover of darkness, are seldom noticed. However, in northern Australia some species live alongside people in houses and are commonly observed perched on walls and window panes where they feed on moths and other flying insects attracted to the lights.

Few reptiles make noises, but geckoes are the exception. In tropical Australian cities the "crk-crk-crk-crk-crk" call of house geckoes is a familiar night sound.

Geckoes have large eyes protected by a clear, fixed spectacle. They regularly clean the eye covering by wiping it with the tongue.

All geckoes have well-developed limbs and each foot has five toes. Tail shape varies between species and may be short and thick, flattened, or long and tapering. Most geckoes will throw off their tail if seized. A new tail eventually regenerates from the stump, but lacks the perfect proportion and markings of the original.

Many geckoes have adhesive pads beneath their toes for walking on smooth surfaces. Some geckoes with highly developed toe pads are able to walk upside down across ceilings and on window glass.

Geckoes are terrestrial or arboreal. During the day they hide in burrows and soil cracks, beneath debris, in rock crevices, under loose bark, within dense grass thickets, or in tree hollows. They emerge after dark to eat small flying and crawling insects, as well as spiders. Some large geckoes prey on smaller geckoes and skinks.

All Australian geckoes are egg-layers and with few exceptions the clutch consists of two eggs.

Top: The Pale Knob-tailed Gecko (*Nephrurus laevissimus*) is an inhabitant of sand-ridge deserts in central and western Australia.

Top: A rock dweller, the beautiful Gracile Velvet Gecko (*Oedura gracilis*) is confined to outcrops and gorges in the rugged Kimberley region of Western Australia. **Above:** The Southern Banded-tailed Gecko (*Phyllurus caudiannulatus*) is confined to two small areas of State forest in central eastern Queensland; it lives on large fig trees in rainforests.

Ring-tailed Gecko

Cyrtodactylus louisiadensis

The Ring-tailed Gecko is Australia's largest and most aggressive gecko and will readily bite if handled roughly. It occasionally dwells on the exterior walls of houses close to native bushland, as well as in sheds and abandoned buildings. An individual has been observed to leap from a wall onto the ground to seize a smaller gecko and return to its elevated position to eat it.

DESCRIPTION: This robust gecko has a large head and moderately long, slender tail. Its body shape is slightly flattened from above. The body scales are small and there are many low, rounded tubercles on the back. The toes are equipped with strong, bird-like claws. The colour of the back and sides is cream to fawn with broad brown crossbands and these bands are enhanced by dark edges. The first crossband curves backwards across the nape from one eye to another. The tail is whitish with contrasting black-brown bands. The undersurface is whitish.

HABITAT: The Ring-tailed Gecko is an inhabitant of rainforest, monsoon forest and humid woodland. It is primarily arboreal, but is also known to live in caves and crevices of outcropping rock.

BEHAVIOUR: The Ring-tailed Gecko shelters by day in hollows of large trees or in crevices and caves in rock outcrops. It emerges after dark to forage on the tree trunk or rock face.

BREEDING: Little is known, but a captive Ring-tailed Gecko laid two hard-shelled eggs and these hatched after a nine month incubation.

ABUNDANCE: Uncommon

DIET: Crickets, cockroaches, moths and spiders, also frogs and smaller geckoes

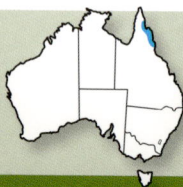

SIZE: Average total length 25 cm, maximum 34 cm

STATUS: Secure

Fat-tailed Gecko

Diplodactylus conspicillatus

The Fat-tailed Gecko shelters by day in an abandoned spider hole. It enters the burrow head first and uses its robust tail to plug the shaft behind it, tucking the tail tip back towards the body to perfect the seal. This deters smaller predators from entering and also helps maintain burrow moisture levels — and gives it the alternative name of "Burrow-plug Gecko". A regenerated tail may be fatter and even better as a plug.

DESCRIPTION: This stout gecko has a very short, thick, slightly flattened tail, which acts as a fat-storage organ. Its body scales are small and smooth and the tail has larger scales and low conical tubercles. The toes have small retractable claws and poorly developed pads. The colour of the back and sides is yellowish-grey to reddish-brown with scattered pale spots and small dark spots, often forming an obscure net-like pattern. A pale streak usually runs from nostril to eye. Its underparts are white.

HABITAT: This species occupies a variety of environments from humid woodland to sparsely vegetated, dry stony or sandy plains.

BEHAVIOUR: After resting in a burrow in the daytime, this gecko emerges at night to forage on open ground nearby. When agitated it may raise and wriggle its short tail while lowering its head. Sometimes it forms its body into a tight coil with the head tucked underneath.

BREEDING: A female Fat-tailed Gecko lays two (occasionally one) eggs per clutch and may produce two clutches each season.

ABUNDANCE: Common
DIET: Small insects, particularly termites

SIZE: Average total length 8 cm
STATUS: Secure

With its distinctive and attractive pattern, the Helmeted Gecko is unmistakeable and readily identified. Its pattern provides an excellent camouflage against the gravel-strewn terrain of its habitat. The fleshy tail of the Helmeted Gecko is a fat store for periods of inactivity.

DESCRIPTION: The robust body of this gecko is covered with small, smooth scales and it has a moderately short, fleshy tail. The toes have small retractable claws and pads. The colour of the back and sides is yellowish-brown to reddish-brown with large, dark-edged, fawn blotches spaced along the body and extending onto the tail. The top of the head is fawn and edged at the base by a dark line curving backwards from one eye to the other. The sides and limbs have a scattering of small white spots. The undersurface is white.

HABITAT: The Helmeted Gecko inhabits rocky slopes in dry woodland or arid shrubland and grassland.

BEHAVIOUR: The Helmeted Gecko emerges from cover to forage on the surface at night. In mild weather it shelters beneath surface rocks during the day. In the hotter months of summer it seeks more substantial cover, beneath a large rock slab or in an abandoned spider hole or deep crevice.

BREEDING: A female Helmeted Gecko lays two eggs per clutch.

ABUNDANCE: Uncommon
DIET: Small invertebrates

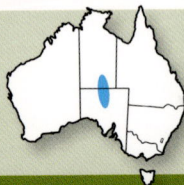

SIZE: Average total length 9 cm
STATUS: Secure

Eastern Stone Gecko *Diplodactylus vittatus*

The geckoes of the large and widespread genus Diplodactylus *occur mainly in Australia's arid regions. The Eastern Stone Gecko is the sole member of its genus to occur in cool, high rainfall areas of south-eastern Australia.*

DESCRIPTION: The Eastern Stone Gecko is robust, with a moderately short, fleshy tail. Its scales are small and smooth. The toes have small retractable claws and pads. The colour of the back and sides is a shade of brown. A ragged or wavy, fawn or pale greyish stripe along the middle of the back widens to encompass the top of the head. This extends in the opposite direction onto the tail, where it separates into a number of blotches. Occasionally this stripe is broken or partly broken into a line of diamond-shaped blotches along the body. The sides are scattered with small pale spots. The undersurface is whitish, with darker peppering.

HABITAT: The Eastern Stone Gecko occurs on sandy plains in dry woodland and rocky areas in dry sclerophyll forest.

BEHAVIOUR: Rocks, logs or bark lying on the ground provide cover for the Eastern Stone Gecko during the day, or it may appropriate the burrow of another lizard or spider. It is largely inactive during the winter months and emerges from its retreat to forage on summer nights. When cornered it raises its inflated body on extended legs and with mouth opened, makes short lunges at its tormentor.

BREEDING: A female Eastern Stone Gecko lays two eggs per clutch.

ABUNDANCE: Common
DIET: Small invertebrates

SIZE: Average total length 9 cm
STATUS: Secure

The Northern Dtella commonly inhabits houses in tropical northern Australia. It chooses to live in and on human dwellings because of the availability of food in the form of moths and other flying insects that are drawn to the lights at night. It moves effortlessly across window panes and smooth interior walls with the help of specialised adhesive pads beneath its toes. In the past few decades it has been displaced from the suburbs of major towns and cities by the invasive Asian House Gecko (Hemidactylus frenatus).

DESCRIPTION: This gecko is solidly built and the body is somewhat flattened from above. The tail is medium length and slender. The scales are small and smooth. The toes have large pads with claws on all but the inner toe of each foot. The colour of the back and sides is uniform brownish-grey, pale grey to pinkish-white, or with a vague darker, crosswise pattern. The undersurface is whitish. The Northern Dtella changes colour at night, becoming very pale and translucent.

HABITAT: The Northern Dtella inhabits humid woodland and dry sclerophyll forest.

BEHAVIOUR: The Northern Dtella is an arboreal gecko, hiding by day beneath bark or in the hollow of a large tree. It emerges at night to forage on the tree trunk. A large tree may support a number of resident Northern Dtellas, each stationed on its section of tree trunk. Some populations inhabit rock outcrops, but these may ultimately prove to be a separate species.

BREEDING: A female Northern Dtella lays two eggs per clutch.

ABUNDANCE: Very common

DIET: Small invertebrates (moths, crickets and spiders); also licks sap oozing from branches of wattle shrubs

SIZE: Average total length 12 cm

STATUS: Secure

Asian House Gecko *Hemidactylus frenatus*

In Australia, the Asian House Gecko is confined to an environment in and around human habitation. Its disappearance from abandoned settlements suggests that human presence is vital to its survival. Its nocturnal "crk-crk-crk-crk-crk" call is a familiar sound to residents of northern Australia.

DESCRIPTION: This gecko has a moderate body, somewhat flattened from above. The tail is medium length, slender and markedly flattened. The scales are small and smooth and there is a scattering of small conical tubercles on the back. Larger, spiny tubercles are present on the sides of an original tail. The toes have pads and claws. The colour of the back and sides is pale brownish-grey with dark mottling tending to form irregular lengthwise lines. The tail sometimes has a pinkish flush. The undersurface is whitish in colour. The Asian House Gecko undergoes a colour change under lights at night, becoming very pale and almost patternless.

HABITAT: The Asian House Gecko lives on and around human dwellings in tropical and sub-tropical northern and eastern Australia.

BEHAVIOUR: The Asian House Gecko dwells within or on the outside of occupied buildings and on trees or amongst debris in suburban gardens. By day it typically shelters behind a picture frame or piece of furniture. At night it takes up a position on a wall, window or screen near a light and feeds on moths, flying ants and termites which are drawn to the light. It moves stealthily to within a few centimetres of its prey and secures it with a sudden lunge.

BREEDING: A female Asian House Gecko lays two hard-shelled eggs in an elevated crevice. The eggs take about 45 days to hatch and the emerging young measure 39 mm in length.

ABUNDANCE: Very common
DIET: Mainly small flying insects

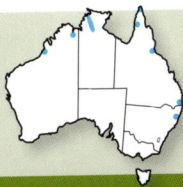

SIZE: Average total length 10 cm
STATUS: Secure

The Prickly Gecko is probably Australia's most widespread and abundant reptile. Some populations are parthenogenetic, consisting entirely of females that reproduce without male participation.

DESCRIPTION: The Prickly Gecko has a moderately robust body with a medium length, slender tail. The scales on the back are granular, with scattered low tubercles often aligned in irregular lengthwise rows. The toes have claws. Body colour and pattern are highly variable: the background colour is grey, yellowish-brown, reddish-brown or dark brown. Fine lighter and darker speckles or larger spots form an irregular crosswise pattern. Occasionally the pattern consists of broad, sharply defined alternating light and dark crossbands. The undersurface is white with darker peppering.

HABITAT: This species occupies an extremely broad range of habitats, including dry shrubland and grassland, woodland, dry sclerophyll forest and coastal forest.

BEHAVIOUR: The terrestrial Prickly Gecko shelters during the day in earth cracks or beneath rocks, fallen timber and other close fitting debris on the ground. It is particularly common under urban rubbish such as discarded sheets of roofing iron. Some populations shelter in crevices of exfoliating rock. At sundown it emerges to forage over a radius of about 10 m from its shelter.

BREEDING: The female Prickly Gecko lays two eggs in a soil crevice or among rocks. Each nest is usually private, but communal nesting sites have been recorded containing up to 150 eggs. Hatchlings stay close until they mature.

ABUNDANCE: Very common

DIET: A variety of small invertebrates; insects and their larvae

SIZE: Average total length 11 cm

STATUS: Secure

When disturbed in the open at night the Beaded Gecko moves quickly to the cover of a low shrub or grass clump. During territorial altercations, males raise their bodies as high as their extended legs will allow and utter chirping noises while positioning themselves to deliver a bite to an adversary.

DESCRIPTION: This gecko has a moderate body with a medium length, slender tail. Its scales are small and smooth. The toes have small claws. The colour of the back and sides is reddish-brown with fine, dark speckling, sometimes forming a net-like pattern. A cream stripe runs along the middle of the back and divides on the nape to form a crown on the head. When this stripe reaches the tail it may separate into blotches. The stripe is sometimes ragged or represented as a line of blotches or "beads". There are cream or white spots on the sides and limbs. The undersurface is white.

HABITAT: The Beaded Gecko is an inhabitant of open sandy plains and dunes, where the vegetation is dry woodland, shrubland or grassland.

BEHAVIOUR: The Beaded Gecko does not dig its own burrow, instead appropriating the abandoned burrow of a spider or small agamid lizard. It rests by day in the burrow and emerges to forage widely in open areas after nightfall. A foraging gecko may travel for a distance of 50 m in one hour.

BREEDING: A female Beaded Gecko lays two (occasionally one) eggs per clutch.

ABUNDANCE: Common

DIET: Small invertebrates including beetles, grasshoppers, moths and spiders

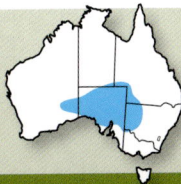

SIZE: Average total length 10 cm

STATUS: Secure

Smooth Knob-tailed Gecko *Nephrurus levis*

The bulky tail of the Smooth Knob-tailed Gecko serves as a fat-store for winter months when the temperature at night is too low for the lizard to remain active. The function of the unique "knob" at the end of its tail is unknown.

DESCRIPTION: This distinctive gecko has a bulky body and a very large head and eyes. Its short turnip-shaped tail is somewhat flattened and terminates with a small spherical knob. The back has a scattering of low spiny tubercles. The limbs are relatively long and the toes have claws. The back and sides are reddish-brown or yellowish-brown with obscure, irregular, purple-brown variegations. Small white spots lie in irregular crosswise rows or join to form narrow crossbands, particularly on the head and nape. The head, nape, hips and tail are often purple-brown. The undersurface is immaculate white.

HABITAT: The Smooth Knob-tailed Gecko occurs on sandy plains and dunes supporting shrubs, spinifex grass and open woodland.

BEHAVIOUR: The ground-dwelling Smooth Knob-tailed Gecko excavates a burrow in sandy soil, or more usually moves into the existing burrow of another lizard or small mammal. The complex burrow of the Night Skink (*Egernia striata*) is often used. It emerges after dark to forage across surrounding plains and dunes.

BREEDING: During the mating embrace, a male Smooth Knob-tailed Gecko climbs onto the female's back and grips the skin of her nape in his jaws. A female lays two eggs per clutch. One female in captivity produced six clutches in one season as a result of a single mating.

ABUNDANCE: Moderately common

DIET: Insects, spiders and smaller geckoes

SIZE: Average total length 12 cm

STATUS: Secure

The small, smooth scales of the Northern Spotted Velvet Gecko impart a "velvety" texture. In response to a threat, it lifts its tail and moves it from side-to-side with a writhing motion. The plump tail serves as a fat store, sustaining the gecko during lean periods.

DESCRIPTION: This attractive gecko is moderately robust and flattened from above. The tail is moderately short, broad and also flattened. Its scales are small and smooth. The toes have small retractable claws and pads. The colour on the back and sides is yellowish with dark-edged, creamish spots aligned in an irregular crosswise pattern. The spots may join to form broken crossbands. Occasionally the dark colouring surrounding the spots forms the background colour. A dark brown stripe extends from the snout, through the eye, to the rear of the head. Juveniles are dark purplish-brown with small yellow spots. The undersurface is whitish.

HABITAT: The Northern Spotted Velvet Gecko inhabits rock outcrops in humid woodland and dry sclerophyll forest.

BEHAVIOUR: The Northern Spotted Velvet Gecko shelters by day beneath exfoliating rock slabs, in deep crevices, or occasionally beneath the loose bark of a nearby fallen tree. It emerges to forage on the rock face at night, sitting motionless and flush with the rock surface awaiting its prey.

BREEDING: A female Northern Spotted Velvet Gecko lays two eggs per clutch.

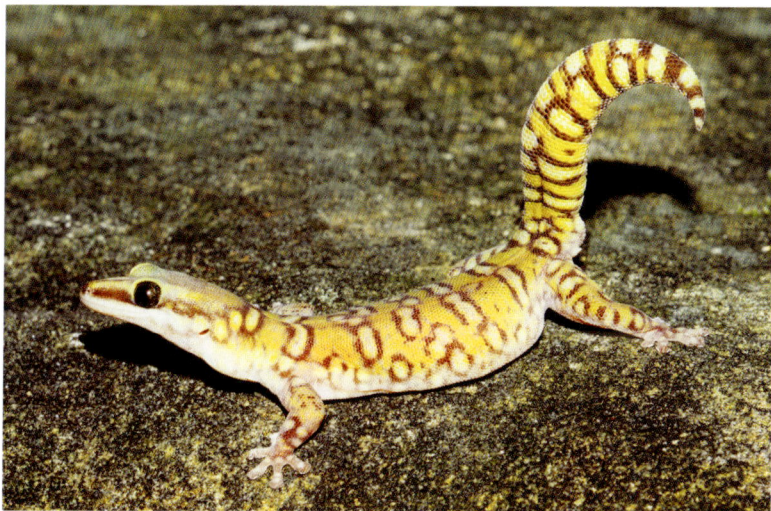

ABUNDANCE: Common
DIET: Insects and spiders

SIZE: Average total length 13 cm
STATUS: Secure

The Marbled Velvet Gecko is a widespread and variable gecko that probably comprises more than one species as currently recognised. It is occasionally encountered on the walls of buildings.

DESCRIPTION: The body of the Marbled Velvet Gecko is moderately robust and flattened from above. The tail is moderately short, broad and also flattened, or in some populations, medium length and more or less rounded. The scales are small and smooth. The toes have small retractable claws and pads. The colour and pattern of the back and sides is variable, but usually mottled purplish-brown and yellow with distinct to obscure creamish or yellow crossbands. The crossbands are usually more pronounced on the tail. A regenerated tail is mottled, without bands. The pattern of an aged gecko often consists of irregular spots and blotches, with little or no indication of a crosswise pattern. Juveniles are purplish-brown with sharply defined bright yellow crossbands. The undersurface is whitish in colour.

HABITAT: This widespread gecko inhabits humid woodland, dry woodland, dry shrubland and grassland, or rocky gorges and outcrops.

BEHAVIOUR: Some populations of Marbled Velvet Geckoes inhabit woodland and shelter by day under loose bark or in cracks and hollows of standing dead trees. Others dwell on rock outcrops and shelter under rock slabs or in deep crevices. Marbled Velvet Geckoes emerge from their retreat on warm nights to forage on the tree trunk or rock face.

BREEDING: A female Marbled Velvet Gecko lays two eggs per clutch.

ABUNDANCE: Common
DIET: Insects, spiders, small geckoes and skinks

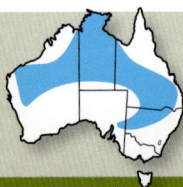

SIZE: Average total length 15 cm
STATUS: Secure

Opposite, top: An adult Marbled Velvet Gecko from Westmar, Qld. **Top:** An adult from Port Hedland, WA. **Above:** The striking colouring and pattern of a juvenile — from Westmar, Qld.

Broad-tailed Rock Gecko   *Phyllurus platurus*

The Broad-tailed Rock Gecko sits flush against a lichen-encrusted rock face and is difficult to detect because of its mottled pattern. It sometimes dwells on brick or stone buildings adjacent to natural habitat.

DESCRIPTION: The body of this gecko looks very flattened from above. A prominent skin fold extends along the side between the forelimb and hindlimb. The head is large and flat; the tail is moderately short, broad and flat, tapering rapidly to a narrow, elongate tip. The limbs are long and thin and the toes have strong, bird-like claws. The head, body, limbs and tail are scattered with spiny tubercles, with the largest forming a fringe on the side of the tail. A regenerated tail is smooth with a shorter tip. The colour of the back and sides is pale brown or greyish with intense dark brown mottling. The undersurface is whitish to pale brownish-grey in colour.

HABITAT: The Broad-tailed Rock Gecko inhabits sandstone rock outcrops in sclerophyll forests.

BEHAVIOUR: The Broad-tailed Rock Gecko shelters during the day in the shaded recesses of a deep crevice. A suitable site may contain as many as sixteen individuals. It emerges at dusk to forage on the walls of wind-blown caves or on vertical rock faces.

BREEDING: A female Broad-tailed Rock Gecko deposits two parchment-shelled eggs in a deep crevice and may lay up to three clutches in one season. A suitable site may be utilised by a number of females and as many as 24 eggs have been recorded from a communal nesting site. Such communal nesting sites are used repeatedly each season.

ABUNDANCE: Common

DIET: Cockroaches, moths, spiders and the smaller Lesueur's Velvet Gecko (*Oedura lesueurii*)

SIZE: Average total length 15 cm

STATUS: Secure

This large and aggressive gecko lunges forward, makes a squeaking noise and bites with determination when cornered. Large adhesive pads beneath the toes and a corresponding pad on the undersurface of the tail tip assist it to manoeuvre on walls and ceilings of caves and overhangs.

DESCRIPTION: This large gecko has a slight flattening of the body from above. The head is large and also moderately flattened. The tail is of medium length, slender and somewhat prehensile. The scales are small and smooth. The toes have large pads and small retractable claws. There is an additional adhesive pad on the undersurface of the tail tip. The colour of the back and sides is reddish-brown to purplish-brown with yellow spots arranged in an irregular crosswise pattern. The yellow spots may merge to form crossbands and these are often offset at the mid-line. An original tail is banded with yellow and dark brown and the regenerated tail is without bands. The undersurface is pinkish in colour.

HABITAT: The Arnhem Land Cave Gecko inhabits precipitous sandstone formations in tropical woodland.

BEHAVIOUR: The Arnhem Land Cave Gecko remains concealed by day in a deep crevice or cave. It is active on open rock faces at night, particularly on steamy summer nights after rainfall. It is an agile gecko, often jumping from one rock to another. During its nocturnal wanderings, it sometimes ventures into the branches of fig trees growing against the cliff face.

BREEDING: A female Arnhem Land Cave Gecko usually lays two eggs (occasionally one) per clutch.

ABUNDANCE: Moderately common

DIET: Cockroaches, moths, spiders and smaller geckoes

SIZE: Average total length 20 cm

STATUS: Secure

29

When threatened or seized, the Northern Spiny-tailed Gecko squirts or smears a sticky, irritant liquid from pores on its tail as a defensive strategy. It lifts its tail and repeatedly ejects fine threads of the syrupy liquid over a short distance to envelope a predator.

DESCRIPTION: This spectacular gecko has a moderately sized body with a relatively short, slender tail. There are two loosely aligned lengthwise rows of conical tubercles on the back. The tail has two more orderly rows of larger spines. There are 2–4 distinctive spines sitting above the eye. The toes have small retractable claws and pads. The colour of the back and sides is variable. The population from the northern Northern Territory is deep reddish-brown in colour with bright orange blotches, scattered white scales and concentrations of white scales forming large blotches on either side of the back. This gecko undergoes a dramatic colour change at night, becoming ghostly white with a few scattered blackish tubercles and orange blotches. Other populations are pale grey with a complex pattern of dark grey variegation and mottling. The undersurface is whitish.

HABITAT: This gecko occurs in humid woodland, dry woodland, or dry shrubland and grassland.

BEHAVIOUR: The Northern Spiny-tailed Gecko shelters by day beneath loose bark on standing trees, in tree hollows, beneath rock slabs or in dense spinifex grass hummocks. It moves from its cover at dusk to forage on the ground.

BREEDING: A female Northern Spiny-tailed Gecko lays two eggs in loose soil. The eggs hatch after an incubation period of 50–70 days.

ABUNDANCE: Common
DIET: A broad range of small invertebrates

SIZE: Average total length 14 cm
STATUS: Secure

Above: Like many geckoes, the Northern Spiny-tailed Gecko undergoes a dramatic colour change at night. The two photos above are of the same gecko shown on the opposite page.

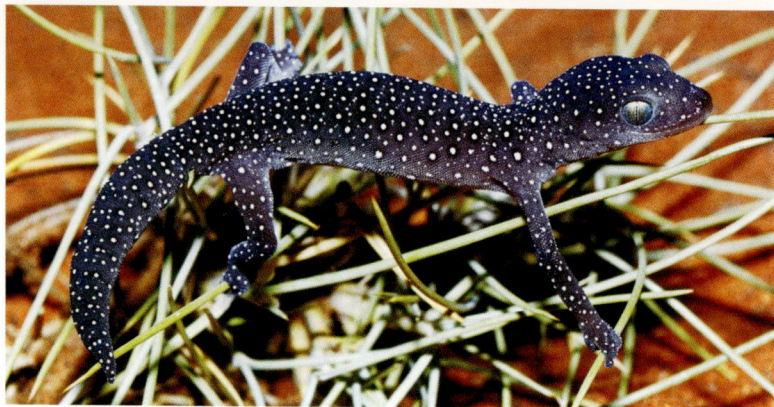

When seized, the Jewelled Gecko emits a sticky irritant liquid from pores on its tail and smears this onto its attacker. Though the lizard-eating Burton's Snake-lizard (Lialis burtonis) is common in spinifex grass, it shuns the unpalatable Jewelled Gecko as a food item.

DESCRIPTION: The Jewelled Gecko has a moderate body with a relatively short, somewhat fleshy tail. The scales of the back and sides are small and smooth, with scattered low tubercles. The toes have small retractable claws and pads. The colour of the back and sides is yellowish-brown, greyish-brown, to dark purplish-brown with evenly distributed, dark-edged, small white spots corresponding to the tubercles. The intensity of the spots varies greatly throughout its range. In some populations the spots are few and widely spaced while in others they are many and densely packed. The undersurface is pale grey with darker speckles.

HABITAT: This attractive gecko occurs on plains, dunes and rocky hills supporting spinifex grass and dry woodland.

BEHAVIOUR: The Jewelled Gecko dwells exclusively in dense spinifex grass hummocks. It manoeuvres with ease among the spiky needles with the aid of its prehensile tail. As many as ten individuals may occupy a large grass hummock. Feeding and most other activities take place within the grass hummock, but Jewelled Geckoes are occasionally encountered on open ground between the hummocks at night.

BREEDING: A female Jewelled Gecko lays two eggs, probably in soil beneath a spinifex grass hummock. In captivity females have produced two clutches per season.

ABUNDANCE: Common
DIET: Small invertebrates

SIZE: Average total length 8 cm
STATUS: Secure

The Thick-tailed Gecko is also called the Barking Gecko. When threatened, it arches its inflated body on fully extended limbs and with its mouth opened wide launches a mock counterattack while emitting a "barking" noise. The impact of this display on a predator contemplating the gecko as its next meal might well determine its fate.

DESCRIPTION: This colourful gecko has a robust body and a large head. Its distinctive tail is moderately short, carrot-shaped and somewhat flattened. The back and sides are scattered with numerous low conical tubercles, and there are larger, spiny tubercles on the tail. The limbs are long and slender and the toes have claws. The colour of the back and sides is purplish-brown, reddish-brown or pinkish. Small yellowish spots are arranged in irregular crosswise rows and correspond with the spiny tubercles. The original tail is black with 5–6 narrow white bands. A regenerated tail is smooth and without bands. The undersurface is white.

HABITAT: The Thick-tailed Gecko inhabits a wide range of environments including dry shrubland and grassland, woodland, dry sclerophyll forest and rock outcrops.

BEHAVIOUR: The Thick-tailed Gecko shelters by day under a rock slab or beneath fallen timber and bark. In sandy regions it often excavates a small side chamber within the burrow of a larger animal such as the rabbit. It emerges from its burrow after dark to forage near its refuge. Small groups of Thick-tailed Geckoes often gather together to share a suitable shelter site.

BREEDING: A female Thick-tailed Gecko lays two eggs and is capable of producing up to three clutches per season.

ABUNDANCE: Common

DIET: Insects, spiders, scorpions and occasionally small lizards

SIZE: Average total length 12 cm

STATUS: Secure

Legless Lizards

Family: Pygopodidae

Not all long, snake-like animals are snakes. Legless lizards lack forelimbs, and though they do have hindlimbs, these are not at all obvious — they are flap-like and usually held against the body. These lizards are only found in Australia (which is home to 38 species) and New Guinea.

Legless lizards move in a snake-like manner and are easily confused with snakes when seen in the bush: indeed, some appear to mimic venomous snakes as a defensive strategy. But closer scrutiny reveals many differences. A legless lizard's tail is much longer than any snake's tail and may account for 80 percent of the lizard's total length. A snake's tongue is slender and forked, but that of a legless lizard is wide and flat. Though all legless lizards have remnant hindlimbs, among snakes only pythons have these structures. Snakes have no external ear opening, whereas most legless lizards do. Legless lizards share similarities with geckoes, and may have evolved from this family. Like geckoes they make squeaking sounds, use the tongue to clean their eye shields, lay two eggs and readily cast off their fragile tail when seized.

Legless lizards are secretive and usually move about in the open only at night. However many are day-active in cooler regions. All are terrestrial, but some will climb into shrubs or grass clumps to bask. Some species burrow in loose soil beneath leaf litter, others shelter in dense vegetation or beneath rocks and logs.

These lizards feed mainly on insects and spiders, but also on fruits and nectar. One distinctive species, Burton's Snake-lizard (*Lialis burtonis*), preys on lizards.

Top: The Northern Delma (*Delma borea*) is a common and widespread legless lizard of northern and central Australia.

Top: Like many legless lizards the Plain Delma (*Delma inornata*) has a very long tail. The tail measures more than three times the length of its body. **Above:** The Eastern Hooded Scaly-foot (*Pygopus schraderi*) inhabits dry regions in the eastern half of Australia. It feeds mainly on spiders and scorpions.

The Basalt Delma utters a squeaking sound when disturbed. It will readily cast off its long tail — or a portion of it — to escape the grasp of a predator, but it usually discards only enough of the tail to make its escape. Often the contracting, cast-off tail section is longer than the remaining animal and is more than enough to maintain the attention of a predator.

DESCRIPTION: The Basalt Delma has a slender body and the tail is very long: at least 2–3 times the length of the body. Its scales are smooth. The hindlimb flap is of moderate size and is triangular in shape. The colour of the back and sides is uniform greyish to olive-brown. The top of the head is dark greyish-brown to blackish, or there may be only a blackish bar across the nape. The face and side of the neck are yellowish or rusty brown and this colouring sometimes extends onto the forebody. The lips are marked with black vertical bars. The head pattern is often obscure or absent on adults and more pronounced on juveniles. The undersurface is whitish in colour. The mid-body scales, including two wider ventral scales, are in 14–16 rows.

HABITAT: The Basalt Delma lives in dry sclerophyll forest and humid woodland.

BEHAVIOUR: The Basalt Delma is active during the day and on warm nights. It shelters in earth cracks, spider burrows or beneath rocks, fallen timber or leaf litter. It extends its small hindlimb flaps to assist it while manoeuvring across rough terrain or within dense grass.

BREEDING: A female Basalt Delma lays two eggs per clutch.

ABUNDANCE: Common
DIET: Insects and spiders

SIZE: Average total length 35 cm
STATUS: Secure

The Excitable Delma adopts an ambush position concealed in loose soil or leaf litter with only the head showing. When threatened on open ground it executes a series of frantic jumping movements while progressing towards the nearest cover. The body is lifted from the ground by rapid vertical undulations and thrusts forward as the tail contacts the ground. This bizarre behaviour is intended to confound a predator in pursuit.

DESCRIPTION: The Excitable Delma has a slender body and the tail is very long, more than three times the length of the body. Its scales are smooth. The hindlimb flap is of moderate size and triangular in shape. The colour of the back and sides is yellowish-brown, reddish-brown or greyish-brown. The top of the head is glossy black and traversed by about three narrow yellow crossbands. This head pattern is obscure on adults but strongly contrasting on juveniles. The undersurface is white. The mid-body scales, including two wider ventral scales, are in 12–16 rows.

HABITAT: The Excitable Delma inhabits dry sclerophyll forest, humid woodland, dry woodland, or dry shrubland and grassland.

BEHAVIOUR: The Excitable Delma is active during the day and on warm nights. It shelters in soil beneath leaf litter, within dense grass tussocks, in soil cracks or spider burrows, or beneath rocks, fallen timber and bark.

BREEDING: A female Excitable Delma lays two eggs per clutch.

ABUNDANCE: Common
DIET: Insects and spiders

SIZE: Average total length 30 cm
STATUS: Secure

Burton's Snake-lizard has recurved, snake-like teeth which help it secure a firm grip on the smooth scales of skinks, its main food item.

DESCRIPTION: Burton's Snake-lizard has a somewhat robust body. The head is very long and sharply pointed. The tail is long, about twice the length of the body. The body scales are smooth and the head scales are small and irregular. The hindlimb flap is small. Colour and pattern are highly variable, both geographically and also within populations. The colour of the back and sides is uniform creamish, yellow, light brown, reddish-brown, pale grey to dark grey, or with a series of distinct to obscure lengthwise dashes, or continuous stripes extending the full length of the body and tail. The face is occasionally marbled or often has strongly contrasting white and dark brown stripes extending from the nose through the eye onto the neck. The undersurface is variable, usually a lighter or darker shade of the colour above. The mid-body scales, including two wider ventral scales, are in 18–22 rows.

HABITAT: Burton's Snake-lizard inhabits sclerophyll forests, woodlands, or dry shrubland and grassland.

BEHAVIOUR: Burton's Snake-lizard is active during the day and on warm nights. It is often encountered moving in the open during the first few hours after sundown. It shelters within dense spinifex grass hummocks or beneath rocks and fallen timber.

BREEDING: A female Burton's Snake-lizard lays between one and three (usually two) eggs per clutch.

Top: Burton's Snake-lizards, Bowen, Qld.

ABUNDANCE: Common

DIET: Small lizards, particularly skinks, but also geckoes, other legless lizards and dragons

SIZE: Average total length 45 cm

STATUS: Secure

Above and right: Colour variants of Burton's Snake-lizard in Elliott, NT; And in Kenilworth, Qld. **Top:** Burton's Snake-lizard feeds mainly on skinks.

The Brigalow Scaly-foot is considered vulnerable because of its restricted distribution and the extensive clearing of much of its habitat. When threatened it assumes the posture of a venomous snake, with head and forebody elevated and tongue flickering repeatedly.

DESCRIPTION: The Brigalow Scaly-foot has a somewhat robust body. The tail is long, about twice the length of the body. The hindlimb flap is of moderate size. The scales are smooth and glossy. The colour of the back and sides is brownish-grey to milky, bluish-grey. The sides sometimes have an indication of faint dark lengthwise lines. There is a broad yellow bar on the nape and a narrower blackish bar immediately behind it. A blackish patch surrounds the eye. These markings may be somewhat faded on mature animals. The undersurface is whitish in colour. The mid-body scales, including two wider ventral scales, are in 18–20 rows.

HABITAT: The Brigalow Scaly-foot occurs in dry woodland and on sandstone ridges.

BEHAVIOUR: The Brigalow Scaly-foot is active during the day and on warm nights. It shelters within dense grass clumps or beneath rocks and fallen timber. It has been observed to climb into shrubs to lick sap oozing from branches. A spider too large to swallow is pulverised with repeated bites and the body juices are then lapped up.

BREEDING: A female Brigalow Scaly-foot lays two eggs per clutch.

ABUNDANCE: Uncommon
DIET: Insects, spiders, tree sap

SIZE: Average total length 45 cm
STATUS: Vulnerable

Western Hooded Scaly-foot   *Pygopus nigriceps*

Upon seizing a large spider or scorpion in its jaws, the Western Hooded Scaly-foot rapidly rotates its entire body on a lengthwise axis, presumably to disorientate and batter its prey against the ground. The prey is then crushed in its powerful jaws and the lizard laps up the body juices. Body rotation is also used to escape a predator's grasp.

DESCRIPTION: The Western Hooded Scaly-foot has a somewhat robust body. Its tail is about twice the length of the body. The hindlimb flap is large and paddle-shaped. The scales on the back are smooth. Its pattern varies from prominent to obscure. The colour of the back and sides is generally yellowish-brown with reddish-brown mottling tending to form a net-like or oblique pattern. The top of the tail may have distinct reddish bars. A grey, dark brown or black hood covers the head and neck, or there may be a bar across the head and another on the nape. There is a blackish blotch below the eye. The head pattern is well defined on juveniles and often obscure on adults. The undersurface is whitish, and the mid-body scales, including two wider ventral scales, are in 21–25 rows.

HABITAT: This species lives in dry woodland, shrubland and grassland.

BEHAVIOUR: The Western Hooded Scaly-foot is primarily nocturnal, but occasionally active by day in the morning and afternoon. It shelters beneath rocks and fallen timber, within dense spinifex grass hummocks, and in soil cracks and abandoned burrows.

BREEDING: A female Western Hooded Scaly-foot lays two eggs per clutch.

ABUNDANCE: Common
DIET: Insects, scorpions, spiders and their egg sacs

SIZE: Average total length 40 cm
STATUS: Secure

When cornered, the Southern Scaly-foot raises its forebody high from the ground, flattens its neck and flicks out its tongue, mimicking the threat behaviour of some venomous snakes.

DESCRIPTION: The Southern Scaly-foot has a somewhat robust body. Its tail is long, more than twice the length of the body. The hindlimb flap is large and paddle-shaped. The scales on the back and sides are strongly keeled. The colour of the back and sides is uniform greyish-brown or reddish-brown and it has a pale grey head, neck and latter portion of the tail. Some animals have small brown to blackish dashes aligned lengthwise and wavy streaks on the head and neck. In the western extremity of its range, the pattern consists of alternating black and pale brown dashes forming continuous lines along the body. The undersurface is pale grey with darker variegation. The mid-body scales, including two wider ventral scales, are in 21–25 rows.

HABITAT: The Southern Scaly-foot lives in sclerophyll forest, woodland, heath, or dry shrubland and grassland.

BEHAVIOUR: The Southern Scaly-foot is mainly diurnal, but also active on warm nights. It shelters within dense grass clumps or beneath rocks and fallen timber. It basks, often on top of grass clumps or low shrubs, in the hours of the morning and afternoon when the sun is not at full strength.

BREEDING: Lays two eggs per clutch. Communal nesting sites are sometimes encountered and one such site contained 76 eggs.

ABUNDANCE: Common
DIET: Insects, spiders, scorpions and some fruits

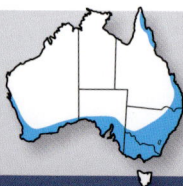

SIZE: Average total length 50 cm
STATUS: Secure

Top: Southern Scaly-foot, coastal eastern Australia.
Above: Southern Scaly-foot, south-western Australia.

Dragons
Family: Agamidae

About 70 species of dragons occur in Australia and they reach their greatest diversity in the dry central regions of the continent. Dragons spend much of the day basking in sunshine to maintain a high body temperature. This is necessary if they are to remain alert and move quickly to escape predators or catch prey.

All dragons have moveable eyelids, four strongly clawed limbs and usually a long, tapering tail. The skin is often rough, with spiny scales. Some distinctive species have large spines, crests, or an extendable gular pouch or frill. This adornment, together with a threatening posture, is a warning to predators or rival males. Dragons have excellent vision and are particularly attracted to movement. A dragon typically sits on a tree stump or other elevated perch and jumps to the ground to seize a passing insect when it wanders into its field of view. Some dragons also eat flowers and fruits.

Unlike most other lizards, male and female dragons of many species differ in appearance. Typically, males have a more colourful pattern than females, particularly in the breeding season. They are also larger, more robust or have larger spines than females. Many dragons change colour in response to temperature variation, becoming pale when warm and darker when cold.

Dragons often use visual signals when interacting with each other or a potential predator. These might include head-bobbing and arm-waving — behaviour that is unknown in other lizard families. Signalling is most intense during the breeding season when one male encroaches on another's territory.

The majority of dragons are terrestrial, living in a burrow in the soil, or in a rock crevice. Many are arboreal and climb among shrubs and trees. The semi-aquatic Water Dragon (*Physignathus lesueurii*) lives along rivers and creeks and plunges into the water to escape predators.

All Australian dragons lay eggs. A female digs a burrow into the soil, deposits her eggs in a chamber at its end and then backfills the nest.

Top: A mature male Northern Water Dragon (*Amphibolurus temporalis*) develops strongly contrasting colours in the breeding season.
Opposite: A male Bennett's Two-lined Dragon (*Diporiphora bennettii*) perches on a termite mound to enhance its view. When an insect appears, it leaps to the ground, seizes its prey and returns to its vantage point.

The Frilled Lizard enacts a remarkable defensive display when threatened. With its mouth agape, displaying the bright yellow interior and the erect frill encircling its head, it stands largely on its hindlimbs while rocking from side-to-side and hissing loudly. At the first opportunity it runs on its hindlimbs to the safety of a nearby tree.

DESCRIPTION: The Frilled Lizard has a robust body with a large, angular head and long limbs. Its tail is moderately long and slender. The scales of the back are mostly keeled. The large, paper-thin frill encircles the head at right angles to the body when erect and is folded back against the neck and forebody when at rest. The colour of the back and sides is grey, blackish, yellowish-brown or reddish-brown with darker mottling or variegation, often defining large pale blotches. This pattern is prominent on juveniles and obscure to virtually absent on most adults. Mature males from the north-west of its range have reddish-orange on the frill and sometimes black on the face and frill. In eastern Australia males are yellowish and more sombre in colour. The undersurface is white to yellowish or black on mature males.

HABITAT: The arboreal Frilled Lizard inhabits dry woodland, humid woodland and dry sclerophyll forest.

BEHAVIOUR: The Frilled Lizard rests on branches or in hollows in the treetops for much of the northern dry season (winter). It is active in the wet season (summer) descending to the ground, often after rain, to feed.

BREEDING: A female Frilled Lizard lays about ten eggs per clutch.

ABUNDANCE: Common

DIET: Insects, including termites, also spiders and occasionally small lizards

SIZE: Average total length 75 cm

STATUS: Secure

Opposite, top: Frilled Lizard, Proserpine, Qld. **Top:** Frilled Lizard, Darwin, NT.
Above: A hatchling Frilled Lizard relies on its cryptic pattern to avoid predators.

A male Tawny Dragon directs a spectacular territorial display towards a rival male. After taking up a prominent position on an elevated rock, it lifts its body, erects its nuchal crest, lowers its gular pouch and coils the tail horizontally.

DESCRIPTION: The Tawny Dragon is somewhat robust and the head and body are strongly flattened from above. Its tail is moderately long and slender. The scales on the back are weakly keeled and there are a few slightly larger tubercles scattered on the sides. Enlarged strongly keeled scales form a low erectable nuchal crest. Males and females differ markedly in appearance. Males often have vivid colours, females are more sombre. Colour and pattern, particularly that of males, varies markedly between populations. Males are dark bluish-grey to brown above.

The sides are blackish above and blue below. Orange or yellow streaks, variegations and spots adorn the face, throat, neck and forebody. Females are mottled greyish-brown to reddish-brown with a broad blackish zone on the upper sides. The undersurface is whitish to grey with darker mottling on the chin and throat.

HABITAT: The Tawny Dragon lives on rock outcrops in woodland, dry shrubland and grassland.

BEHAVIOUR: The Tawny Dragon is an active, sun-loving lizard. It retreats beneath a rock slab or into a narrow rock crevice when alarmed.

BREEDING: A female Tawny Dragon lays about five eggs per clutch and the young hatch after an incubation period of about 60 days. The hatchlings are very secretive and dwell on the fringe of the rock outcrop away from the adults.

ABUNDANCE: Common
DIET: Small invertebrates, including spiders, ants and other insects

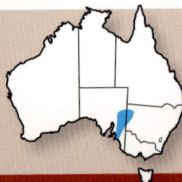

SIZE: Average total length 20 cm
STATUS: Secure

Central Military Dragon

Ctenophorus isolepis

The Military Dragon gets its common name due to the resemblance of its pattern to a military uniform.

DESCRIPTION: The Central Military Dragon has a medium build. The head and body are somewhat flattened from above. The tail is moderately long and slender. The scales of the back are keeled, becoming smooth on the sides. Males and females differ in appearance. The male is rich reddish-brown above with black spots and small whitish, dark-edged blotches in a lengthwise alignment. There is black colouring on the face, side of the neck and sides. The lips are white or bright yellow. A narrow whitish or yellow stripe extends along the edge of the back, from the neck onto the tail, or it may be broken to form a series of spots. The undersurface is white with black on the chin, throat, abdomen and limbs. Females have a more sombre colour and pattern.

HABITAT: The terrestrial Central Military Dragon inhabits open dry woodland or dry shrubland and grassland, particularly in sandy areas with an abundance of spinifex grass. It does not climb onto an elevated perch, like most dragons.

BEHAVIOUR: The Central Military Dragon is a swift moving, sun loving lizard. It forages on open ground between spinifex grass hummocks and darts quickly into this spiky sanctuary when threatened. It shelters deep within the spinifex grass to escape the intense heat of the midday sun.

BREEDING: A female Central Military Dragon lays about four eggs per clutch. Central Military Dragons are short-lived. Hatchlings reach maturity after one year and following breeding, rarely survive to reproduce in the next season.

ABUNDANCE: Common
DIET: Small invertebrates, particularly ants

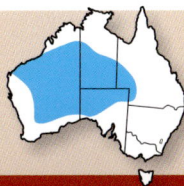

SIZE: Average total length 18 cm
STATUS: Secure

The Central Netted Dragon is an abundant, widespread dragon with a preference for open areas. It changes its colour in relation to its body temperature. In the morning when its body is cool it is dark in colour. As it basks and its body warms up, it becomes progressively lighter. A common and conspicuous lizard, the Central Netted Dragon is preyed upon by many animals including snakes, monitor lizards, birds-of-prey, dingoes and feral cats.

DESCRIPTION: The Central Netted Dragon has a robust body, blunt bulky head and a medium-length tail. The scales of the back and sides are small and more or less smooth with a few small, low tubercles. It has a low, spiny nuchal crest. The colour of the back and sides is yellow to reddish-brown with an intense dark brown net-like pattern. There is a narrow yellowish line running along the middle of the back. The tail usually has obscure dark brown bars or blotches on the sides. A breeding male has an orange flush on the head and throat. The undersurface is white, usually with grey variegation on the throat.

HABITAT: The Central Netted Dragon inhabits open dry woodland or dry shrubland and grassland.

BEHAVIOUR: The Central Netted Dragon digs a shallow burrow in sandy soil and perches close by on fallen timber, a termite mound or low shrub. When approached it quickly retreats to the safety of its burrow, which it also uses to escape the extreme midday heat. A single lizard may have multiple burrows to choose from within its home range.

BREEDING: A female Central Netted Dragon lays 3–4 eggs per clutch.

ABUNDANCE: Common
DIET: Small invertebrates, plants and occasionally small lizards

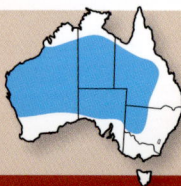

SIZE: Average total length 25 cm
STATUS: Secure

Painted Dragon *Ctenophorus pictus*

A mature male Painted Dragon is one of Australia's most colourful lizards. Hatchlings and sub-adult males are similar in appearance to females and do not develop their spectacular colouration until they reach maturity.

DESCRIPTION: The Painted Dragon has a medium build and the tail is fairly long and slender. The scales of the back are small, smooth to weakly keeled and slightly enlarged along the backbone. Both the nuchal crest and vertebral ridge are erectable. Males and females differ markedly in appearance. Breeding males have vibrant, contrasting colours. The male is red to brown above with blackish flecks, often forming a net-like pattern, and with small cream spots in an irregular crosswise alignment. The vertebral ridge is black with white spots or bars. The throat, lower flanks and sides of the tail are blue. His head is reddish or yellow and the chest is yellow. Females are similarly patterned but are duller brown and lack the blue and yellow. The undersurface is white.

HABITAT: This species inhabits dry open woodland or shrubland and grassland.

BEHAVIOUR: The Painted Dragon perches on fallen timber or rocks and retreats to a short burrow at the base of a low shrub or spinifex grass hummock when threatened.

BREEDING: A female Painted Dragon lays about four eggs per clutch.

Top: Female Painted Dragon. **Above:** Mature male Painted Dragon.

ABUNDANCE: Common
DIET: Small invertebrates, particularly ants

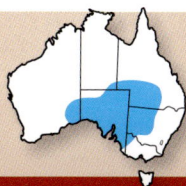

SIZE: Average total length 16 cm
STATUS: Secure

A male Red-barred Dragon performs a stunning territorial display, lifting its body, erecting its nuchal crest and vertebral ridge, lowering its gular pouch and holding its tail in a vertical coil.

DESCRIPTION: This spectacular dragon has a somewhat robust build and the head and body are flattened from above. Its tail is moderately long and slender. The scales of the back are weakly keeled, with larger strongly keeled scales forming a moderate nuchal crest, continuous with a low vertebral ridge. Both the nuchal crest and vertebral ridge are erectable. Males and females differ markedly in appearance. Males have vivid colours, females are more sombre. Males are bluish-grey to bright blue on the limbs, tail and vertebral region. The back and sides are blackish with an irregular reddish or orange crosswise pattern. There is a yellow flush at the side of the neck and yellow spots on the lower flanks. Females are brown with lighter and darker speckles forming a vague crosswise pattern. The undersurface of the male is whitish with bluish-grey markings on the chest, throat and limbs, and yellow on the throat and chest. The undersurface of the female is whitish with grey streaks on the chin and throat.

HABITAT: The Red-barred Dragon inhabits rock outcrops in dry open woodland or shrubland and grassland.

BEHAVIOUR: A male Red-barred Dragon perches on a prominent, elevated site among rocks and vigorously defends its territory from other males. When alarmed, it retreats to a narrow crevice.

ABUNDANCE: Common
DIET: Small invertebrates

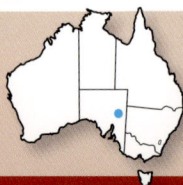

SIZE: Average total length 26 cm
STATUS: Secure

The bright colouring of a breeding male Yellow-sided Two-lined Dragon can change rapidly to dull grey.

DESCRIPTION: This dragon has a medium build and a moderately long, slender tail. The scales on the back are keeled, and enlarged keeled scales form a low nuchal crest. The colour of the back and sides of females and subadults is brownish with a series of dark brown bars straddling the vertebral zone. These are interrupted by a narrow grey vertebral stripe and a cream stripe either side. A narrow pale stripe is often present on the flanks. This pattern may become obscure with age. Breeding males have little or no pattern apart from distinct yellow stripes on either side of the vertebral region. The body and tail are olive-green to bright yellow and the head and neck are pale grey. There is a large black patch above the forelimb. The undersurface is whitish.

HABITAT: The Yellow-sided Two-lined Dragon is an inhabitant of woodland.

BEHAVIOUR: The Yellow-sided Two-lined Dragon perches on fallen timber, rocks, termite mounds or in low shrubs. When disturbed it retreats beneath a log or rock, or into a dense shrub.

Top: Male Yellow-sided Two-lined Dragon in breeding colours. **Above:** Female Yellow-sided Two-lined Dragon.

ABUNDANCE: Common
DIET: Small invertebrates

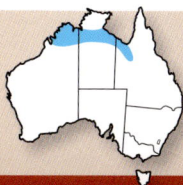

SIZE: Average total length 24 cm
STATUS: Secure

Boyd's Forest Dragon is a slow-moving lizard that relies heavily on camouflage to avoid predators. It perches in an upright position on the trunk of a sapling and shuffles silently around to the other side when approached.

DESCRIPTION: Boyd's Forest Dragon has a robust body and a large, angular head. The body is somewhat flattened at the sides. Its tail is long and slender with a blunt tip. The scales of the back and sides are keeled with scattered enlarged spiny scales on the sides. It has a high nuchal crest with very large flattened tooth-like spines. Large flattened spines also form a prominent vertebral ridge. The deep extendable gular pouch is edged with white flattened spines. The colour of the back and sides is mottled olive-green or greyish, often with a crosswise pattern of obscure broad pale bars and narrow dark bars. The tail has obscure broad dark bars. The face is bluish-grey with large white disc-like scales on the cheeks. A blackish patch on the side of the neck is dissected by a white horizontal bar. There is a yellow flush on the throat and behind the eye. The undersurface is whitish to pale brown.

HABITAT: Boyd's Forest Dragon is an inhabitant of tropical rainforest.

BEHAVIOUR: This spectacular Dragon basks where a break in the canopy allows sunlight to filter through to the forest floor. It forages in the lower canopy and on the ground and shelters in a tree hollow or beneath a log. Boyd's Forest Dragon often sleeps exposed on the trunk of a sapling on warm summer nights.

BREEDING: A female Boyd's Forest Dragon lays about five eggs per clutch and may produce multiple clutches in a season. A captive female was observed to position her eggs in a cavity with her snout.

ABUNDANCE: Uncommon

DIET: Invertebrates including cockroaches, crickets, spiders and earthworms

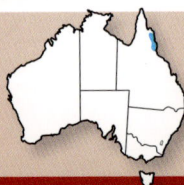

SIZE: Average total length 45 cm

STATUS: Secure

A Thorny Devil can drink by simply standing in a puddle or on wet sand. Water is soaked up by capillary action and moves from the limbs, along a network of fine channels between the scales, to the corners of the mouth.

DESCRIPTION: The Thorny Devil is a distinctive and unmistakeable lizard. It has a robust body and the small blunt head has a very large spine above each eye. The tail is moderately short and thick with a blunt tip. The scales of the back and sides are granular with a mass of large spines jutting from the head, body, limbs and tail. A distinct spiny hump on the nape has a very large spine at either side. The colour of the back and sides is dark brown to reddish-brown with irregular yellow cross-bars. A thin white vertebral line and another on either side of the back extend from the back of the neck to the tail tip. There is a broad yellow stripe from the eye to the forebody. The tail is brown with broad irregular white cross-bars and the limbs are whitish. The undersurface has a reddish marbled pattern.

HABITAT: The Thorny Devil inhabits dry woodland, dry shrubland and grassland.

BEHAVIOUR: The Thorny Devil shelters at night and during the hottest part of the day beneath a shrub, under the overhang of hummock grass or in a shallow burrow. It is most active in the early morning and late afternoon, particularly on overcast days. Although slow-moving, a determined Thorny Devil can cover a distance of over 500 metres in a day.

BREEDING: A female Thorny Devil digs a substantial burrow in sandy soil for her eggs. The burrow is about 50 cm long. The female works for several days to excavate and backfill the nesting burrow. She lays from 3–10 eggs in a small chamber at the end of the burrow.

ABUNDANCE: Uncommon

DIET: Feeds exclusively on small ants, consuming up to 5000 per meal with a rapid flicking of its tongue

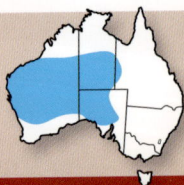

SIZE: Average total length 18 cm

STATUS: Secure

Opposite, top: A Thorny Devil basks in late afternoon sunshine. **Top and above:** The Thorny Devil moves across the red sands with a slow, jerking motion.

Water Dragon *Physignathus lesueurii*

The Water Dragon is arboreal and semi-aquatic, typically dropping from an overhanging branch into the water when approached.

DESCRIPTION: The Water Dragon has a large, deep head and a robust body, somewhat flattened at the sides. The tail is long, slender and flattened at the sides. The scales of the back and sides are small and keeled, with larger spiny scales strung in an irregular crosswise alignment. The gular pouch is extendable. Large spiny scales form an erectable nuchal crest and a spiny ridge extends along the backbone to the tail. Two subspecies exist. Male Eastern Water Dragons (*Physignathus lesueurii lesueurii*) are yellow-brown on the back and sides with black saddles across the back. The face and cheeks are whitish, and a broad black streak extends from the eye to the back of the head. Limbs are black with pale spots and the tail has broad blackish bars. Some populations have a red chest or yellow on face and throat. Male Gippsland Water Dragons (*Physignathus lesueurii howittii*) are bluish-green in colour with yellow mottling on the throat and no red on the chest. Females and juveniles are fairly uniform brown with a subtle pattern and pale brown underparts.

HABITAT: Water Dragons live on rivers and creeks in woodlands, sclerophyll forests, rainforest and also farmland.

BEHAVIOUR: On warm nights, this lizard may sleep on a branch or in the water with only its nostrils above the surface. In colder months it shelters in a burrow below tree roots or a rock. It can remain underwater for up to an hour.

BREEDING: A female Water Dragon selects a sunny position and excavates a nest burrow in the soil about 10 cm deep. From 6–18 eggs are deposited into the nest. An egg mislaid on the surface may be rolled into the nest with the snout or picked up and carried in the mouth. She then backfills the nest and disguises it by raking litter across the surface.

ABUNDANCE: Common

DIET: Feeds on invertebrates including insects, snails, worms and yabbies, plus fish, frogs, small reptiles and fruits

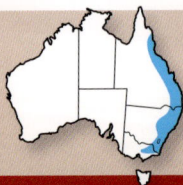

SIZE: Average total length 75 cm

STATUS: Secure

Opposite, top: An adult male Gippsland
Water Dragon (*Physignathus lesueurii howittii*).
Above: An adult male Eastern Water Dragon
(*Physignathus lesueurii lesueurii*).

The Eastern Bearded Dragon, also known as the Frilly Lizard or Jew Lizard, is an abundant and familiar lizard of eastern Australia. Its defensive posture when cornered consists of flattening and tilting the body towards its antagonist, opening the mouth and extending the "beard".

DESCRIPTION: The Eastern Bearded Dragon has a robust body, somewhat flattened from the top. Its head is broad, triangular and also somewhat flattened. The tail is moderately long and slender. The scales of the back and sides are irregular and spiny. The gular pouch forms a prominent "beard" when extended. Enlarged spiny scales are apparent across the base of the head. There is a fringe of long spiny scales on the edge of the "beard" and along the sides of the body. The colour of the back and sides is more or less uniform yellowish, brown, grey or blackish, or with a series of pale blotches along either side of the back. The throat and latter section of the tail are often blackish. The undersurface is whitish or grey, marked with dark oval-shaped rings or dashes.

HABITAT: The Eastern Bearded Dragon inhabits woodlands and dry sclerophyll forest. It is common in suburban and agricultural areas.

BEHAVIOUR: The Eastern Bearded Dragon characteristically basks on a fence post or tree stump and descends to the ground to feed. On warm nights it rests exposed on a tree branch, or shelters in a burrow under fallen timber or beneath loose bark.

BREEDING: A female Eastern Bearded Dragon lays about 20 (occasionally up to 35) eggs per clutch. These are deposited at the end of a shallow burrow that she digs in the soil.

ABUNDANCE: Common

DIET: Feeds on insects, spiders, worms, small lizards and some plants, particularly dandelion flowers

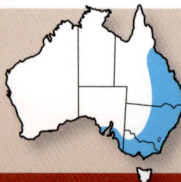

SIZE: Average total length 50 cm

STATUS: Secure

When approached, the Pebble Earless Dragon avoids detection by crouching motionless, with its limbs tucked close to its body, among scattered stones. Its body colour matches the colour of adjacent pebbles and this provides a very effective camouflage. The tail, which is often held at an angle to the body, resembles a short twig and the body is just one more pebble on the plain. If forced to flee, it runs quickly for a short distance, stops abruptly and crouches. This behaviour may cause a predator in pursuit to lose sight of the crouching lizard.

DESCRIPTION: The Pebble Earless Dragon has a very robust body with a short, deep head and short limbs. Its tail is medium length, slender and rapidly tapering from the base. The scales of the back are small, with larger conical tubercles in a loose crosswise alignment. The ear is hidden, covered by scales. The colour of the back and sides is more or less uniform mottled yellowish-brown or reddish-brown, or sometimes with obscure darker blotches or broad bands. A narrow pale vertebral stripe and another on either side may be present on the back. The tail often has distinctive black, whitish and brown blotches or bands. The undersurface is white in colour.

HABITAT: The Pebble Earless Dragon inhabits dry woodland, dry shrubland and grassland and particularly gibber plains or stony hills.

BEHAVIOUR: The Pebble Earless Dragon perches on low rocks or fallen timber. At night it shelters in a short burrow, often beneath its perch site. The Pebble Earless Dragon thrives in an extremely harsh terrain and is very tolerant of high temperatures.

ABUNDANCE: Uncommon
DIET: Small invertebrates, particularly ants

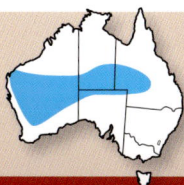

SIZE: Average total length 11 cm
STATUS: Secure

Monitors
Family: Varanidae

Monitors are fast-moving diurnal hunters that feed on almost any animal they are able to overpower. Like snakes, they often swallow very large animals in relation to their body size. Some monitors also eat carrion. Lace Monitors (*Varanus varius*) haunt camping grounds looking for food scraps, or pull entrails from road-killed animals.

A foraging monitor finds food by constantly flicking out its snake-like tongue. The tongue picks up minute airborne particles and these are transferred to a sensory organ in the roof of the mouth for analysis.

Monitors are popularly called "goannas" in Australia, and include our largest and most conspicuous lizards. At a length of 2.4 m, the Perentie (*Varanus giganteus*) is the largest — although until around 25,000 years ago, a huge monitor, *Megalania prisca,* up to 7 m long, roamed the land and its fossils are found today. But some other monitors are small and secretive. The Short-tailed Monitor (*Varanus brevicauda*) is fully grown at 20 cm and is the world's smallest monitor. Australia is home to 26 monitors, about half of the world's known species.

Most monitors live on the ground and shelter within a burrow or narrow rock crevice. Some spend much of their time in trees. Mitchell's Water Monitor (*Varanus mitchelli*) is semi-aquatic, and basks on an overhanging pandanus branch at the river's edge, ready to drop into the water when approached.

A large monitor like the Yellow-spotted Monitor (*Varanus panoptes*), has few natural enemies and often displays indifference at the approach of a human. Even when threatened it is reluctant to retreat, instead adopting a defiant posture with its forebody raised from the ground.

All monitors lay eggs and these are deposited in a burrow excavated by the female in the soil, in hollow decomposing logs, or in an active termite mound.

Top: At a length of almost two metres, the Yellow-spotted Monitor (*Varanus panoptes*) is one of Australia's largest lizards. It lifts its forebody from the ground and stands its ground when confronted. **Opposite:** The Spotted Tree Monitor (*Varanus scalaris*) occurs across northern Australia. It is an arboreal monitor, sheltering in a hollow tree limb, but it regularly descends to the ground to feed.

It is virtually impossible for a predator to dislodge a Spiny-tailed Monitor once it has taken up a position in a narrow rock crevice. It inflates its body and wedges its hard spiny tail firmly in place between the rock surfaces.

DESCRIPTION: The Spiny-tailed Monitor is a moderately robust monitor with short stout legs and a medium length tail. The base of the tail is broadened and somewhat flattened from the top. The scales on the tail have strong spiny keels. A Spiny-tailed Monitor's pattern is usually very distinct, but is occasionally obscure in some populations. The colour of the back and sides is reddish-brown to dark brown with numerous yellow rings in an irregular crosswise alignment. Some of the rings are eye-like, with a brown spot at the centre, or they may join together to form wavy crossbands. Distinctive yellow stripes extend along the face onto the neck. The tail has yellow, usually offset, cross-bands. The undersurface is cream to yellowish in colour.

HABITAT: The Spiny-tailed Monitor inhabits woodlands, dry shrubland and grassland, particularly on stony plains or among outcropping rock.

BEHAVIOUR: The Spiny-tailed Monitor shelters in a burrow in the soil, often beneath a toppled termite mound or flat rock, in holes at the base of a large termite mound, or in a rock crevice. This is a secretive lizard that basks close to its shelter site and slips silently from view when approached.

BREEDING: A female Spiny-tailed Monitor digs a burrow in sandy soil and deposits from 2–11 eggs into a chamber at the end.

ABUNDANCE: Common
DIET: Insects, small lizards and small mammals

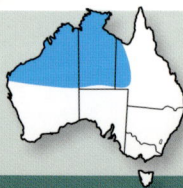

SIZE: Average total length 50 cm
STATUS: Secure

Black-palmed Rock Monitor   *Varanus glebopalma*

This alert monitor sits on an elevated rock ledge and descends swiftly to the ground to seize passing prey. A Black-palmed Rock Monitor has been observed to pursue and capture a dragon lizard over a distance of 30 metres.

DESCRIPTION: The Black-palmed Rock Monitor is a slender monitor with a long neck and long limbs. The tail is long, slender, more or less rounded in section at the base and becoming slightly flattened at the sides. The colour of the back and sides is grey to reddish-brown with pale spots in a crosswise alignment and a coarse blackish net-like pattern that is most prominent on the face and neck. The limbs are blackish with small pale spots. The first half of the tail is blackish and the latter half is yellow. Juveniles have dark grey bands on the yellow tail section. The chest and throat are whitish with a coarse grey net-like pattern. The body pattern of an aged individual is often obscure. The Black-palmed Rock Monitor has distinctive shiny black scales on the soles of its feet. The undersurface is whitish in colour.

HABITAT: The Black-palmed Rock Monitor inhabits rock outcrops in dry sclerophyll forest and woodland.

BEHAVIOUR: The Black-palmed Rock Monitor displays great speed and agility in its rocky environment. In the summer it forages primarily in the cooler hours of early morning and late afternoon. When threatened it swiftly retreats to the safety of a deep rock crevice.

BREEDING: A female Black-palmed Rock Monitor lays about six eggs per clutch.

ABUNDANCE: Uncommon
DIET: Insects, spiders, centipedes, frogs and lizards

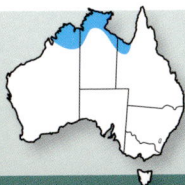

SIZE: Average total length 80 cm
STATUS: Secure

The Perentie is Australia's largest living lizard, and fourth in size globally after the Komodo Dragon, Crocodile Monitor of New Guinea and the Asian Water Monitor. Although it can be swift in retreat, a mature Perentie often stands its ground when approached. It raises its body on stiffened limbs, arches its body and tail, extends the throat and gives a loud, drawn out hiss in warning. At close quarters it will lash its tail and, if further provoked, will readily bite.

DESCRIPTION: The Perentie is a moderately-built monitor with a long neck. Its head has a distinctly angular brow. The tail is long, flattened at the sides and has a prominent dorsal ridge. The colour of the back and sides is brown to blackish with large yellow, dark-edged spots positioned in crosswise rows. The throat, side of the face and the neck are whitish with a coarse blackish net-like marking, and the underparts are the same. The limbs are blackish with yellow spots and the end of the tail is yellow. Patterning tends to be prominent and strongly contrasting, particularly on juveniles.

HABITAT: The Perentie inhabits dry woodland or arid shrubland and grassland, often close to rocky hills.

BEHAVIOUR: The Perentie shelters at night in a deep burrow, often beneath a rock ledge. During the day it forages widely across adjacent plains and dunes.

BREEDING: A female Perentie digs a nesting burrow in sandy soil up to 1.5 m long and lays from 8–13 eggs per clutch. The brightly coloured young hatch some 200–250 days later.

ABUNDANCE: Uncommon
DIET: Invertebrates, reptiles, birds and mammals, also carrion

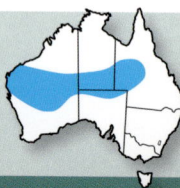

SIZE: Average total length 1.7 m, maximum length 2.4 m
STATUS: Secure

Opposite, top: A Perentie can weigh up to 15 kg.
Top: An adult Perentie has few enemies and will often stand its ground when approached. **Above:** A recently hatched Perentie has a strongly contrasting pattern.

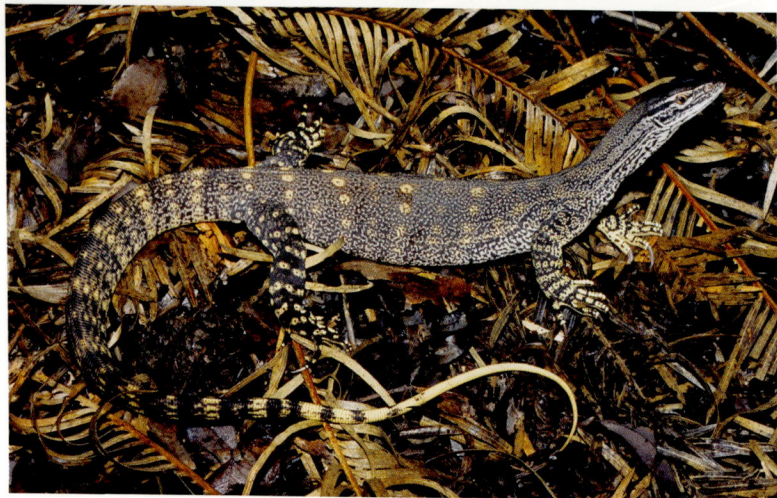

The widespread Sand Monitor is also known as Gould's Monitor, Racehorse Goanna or Bungarra. During the course of a day it might travel more than a kilometre, constantly flicking its tongue, chasing down and seizing small lizards or digging in the soil for frogs and insects.

DESCRIPTION: The Sand Monitor has a medium build. Its moderately long tail is flattened at the sides and has a prominent dorsal ridge. Its pattern is distinct to obscure. The colour of the back and sides is yellowish-brown, reddish-brown to blackish-brown, liberally speckled with yellow. Evenly spaced yellow spots are arranged in a crosswise alignment. A pale-edged, blackish stripe extends from the eye onto the side of the neck. The tail has narrow yellow bands and its last quarter is uniformly yellow. The undersurface is whitish or yellow with scattered darker spots.

HABITAT: The Sand Monitor inhabits arid shrubland and grassland, woodlands and dry sclerophyll forest.

BEHAVIOUR: The Sand Monitor lives in a burrow in sandy soil. It emerges from its burrow in the morning to forage widely in open areas. When threatened, it returns swiftly to its home burrow or any burrow nearby, or it will occasionally scale a tree. If cornered it stands high on its toes, arches its back, inflates its throat and hisses loudly. At close quarters it will lash its tail or bite.

BREEDING: In the wet season (tropics) or spring–summer (temperate areas) a female lays 3–20 eggs per clutch. They may take as long as 230 days to hatch.

ABUNDANCE: Common

DIET: Invertebrates, small vertebrates, eggs and carrion

SIZE: Average total length 1.2 m; some populations are much smaller

STATUS: Secure

Mertens' Water Monitor swims powerfully by holding its limbs flush against the body and using its vertically flattened, paddle-like tail for propulsion through the water. Since the arrival of the poisonous Cane Toad (Rhinella marina, formerly Bufo marinus) in the Northern Territory, Mertens' Water Monitor numbers have suffered a noticeable decline.

DESCRIPTION: Mertens' Water Monitor has a robust body with a moderately long tail. The tail is flattened at the sides and has a high dorsal ridge. The colour of the back and sides is olive, yellowish-brown or blackish-brown with many tiny yellow spots. The lips are pale with bluish-grey bars or mottling and the throat is yellow. The undersurface is whitish or pale yellow with scattered darker spots, bars or a net-like pattern.

HABITAT: Mertens' Water Monitor lives at the edge of billabongs, rivers and creeks, or along rocky gorges, in humid woodland and dry sclerophyll forest.

BEHAVIOUR: Mertens' Water Monitor is semi-aquatic, basking on the river bank or on overhanging vegetation and plunging into the water when approached. Once in the water it may remain submerged for 30 minutes. It often sleeps exposed on a tree branch overhanging the water on warm nights. It forages underwater, walking along the bottom and flicking out its tongue in typical monitor fashion, searching for crustaceans and aquatic insects. In a drying pool, it herds small fish into the shallows against the bank and traps them by forming a barrier with its high tail.

BREEDING: A female Mertens' Water Monitor lays 3–14 eggs into a chamber at the end of a deep nesting burrow in the soil. Hatching is in the wet season.

ABUNDANCE: Common

DIET: Invertebrates, fish, frogs, lizards, birds, mammals and turtle eggs

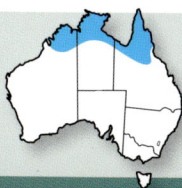

SIZE: Average total length 1 m

STATUS: Secure

Mitchell's Water Monitor *Varanus mitchelli*

This semi-aquatic monitor spends a lot of time in the water foraging for insects, crustaceans and frogs. It swims in the same way as Mertens' Water Monitor. Both species inhabit similar regions of northern Australia, but seem to use the trees and waterways differently.

DESCRIPTION: Mitchell's Water Monitor has a moderately slender build and a long, slender tail. Its tail is strongly flattened at the sides and has a prominent dorsal ridge. The colour of the back and sides is yellowish-brown to reddish-brown with a blackish net-like pattern and numerous small yellow spots. The net-like pattern often encloses a small blackish spot at the centre of each segment, particularly on the forebody. The face, throat and sides of the neck are yellow or orange with dark brown spots and the lips are marked with dark brown bars. The limbs are dark brown with small yellow spots and the tail is more or less uniform dark brown. The undersurface is yellowish with obscure grey bands.

HABITAT: Mitchell's Water Monitor lives along rivers and creeks in humid tropical woodland and dry sclerophyll forest.

BEHAVIOUR: This is a shy lizard. It rests on overhanging vegetation, particularly pandanus, at the water's edge. When approached it shuffles quietly around to the other side of the trunk or drops into the water and hides among debris on the bottom. At night it seeks shelter in a hollow tree limb, and in warm weather, sleeps exposed on a branch overhanging the water.

BREEDING: A female Mitchell's Water Monitor lays about nine eggs per clutch during the dry season.

ABUNDANCE: Common
DIET: Insects, spiders, crustaceans, fish, frogs, lizards and small birds

SIZE: Average total length 50 cm
STATUS: Secure

Heath Monitor *Varanus rosenbergi*

The Heath Monitor is Australia's most southerly ranging and cold-tolerant monitor. Its dark pigmentation allows it to take full advantage of subdued sunshine on winter days or periods of overcast weather.

DESCRIPTION: The Heath Monitor is a somewhat robust monitor with a moderately long tail. The tail is flattened at the sides and has a prominent dorsal ridge. The colour of the back and sides is blackish with very small pale yellow spots concentrated into broad crossbands. A pale-edged black stripe extends from the eye onto the neck. The limbs are blackish with small pale yellow spots and the tail is blackish with narrow pale yellow bands. Hatchlings have orange in place of the pale yellowish colour of an adult. The undersurface is whitish with a grey net-like pattern.

HABITAT: The Heath Monitor is an inhabitant of heath, woodlands and sclerophyll forests.

BEHAVIOUR: The Heath Monitor basks and forages during the day. It shelters at night beneath the ground in a burrow.

BREEDING: A female Heath Monitor digs into an active termite mound and deposits about twelve eggs. The termites, eager to repair the damage, seal off the chamber and provide a secure, temperature-controlled haven for the developing eggs. Heath monitors have been observed digging into termite mounds and subsequently releasing hatchlings, but it is not known if this behaviour is intentional or coincidental.

Below: A brightly coloured hatchling Heath Monitor from Kangaroo Island, SA.

ABUNDANCE: Uncommon

DIET: Invertebrates, frogs, lizards, mammals and birds, also carrion

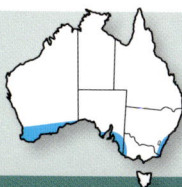

SIZE: Average total length 1.2 m

STATUS: Some populations are considered Vulnerable

Lace Monitor *Varanus varius*

This is the common tree-climbing goanna of eastern Australia and the country's second largest lizard. The Lace Monitor is an opportunistic forager. It climbs trees in search of nestling birds and eggs, takes yabbies and fish from drying waterholes, feeds on the entrails of a road-killed animal or on meat scraps in a picnic ground. It is able to swallow very large prey items. A 1200 g Lace Monitor has been observed to swallow a 500 g rabbit.

DESCRIPTION: The Lace Monitor is a moderately built monitor with a relatively long tail. Its tail is flattened at the sides and has a prominent dorsal ridge. Colour and pattern is intense on juveniles, but sometimes obscure on large adults. The colour of the back and sides is bluish-black with yellow spots of varying sizes arranged in a crossways alignment. Yellow and black bars across the snout extend onto the chin. The tail has broad black and yellow bands. In some parts of the Lace Monitor's range, individuals may have a distinctive pattern consisting of very broad irregular alternate black and yellow bands. Underparts are yellowish with black bands.

HABITAT: This largely arboreal monitor inhabits woodlands, sclerophyll forests and rainforest.

BEHAVIOUR: Foraging takes place in the treetops or on the ground, but an animal quickly scales the nearest tall tree when alarmed. At night it shelters in a tree hollow, or occasionally in a burrow or rock crevice.

BREEDING: A female lays about ten eggs in an active termite nest in a tree or on the ground. She backfills and the termites patch the hole. The young hatch and burrow out after a long incubation period of up to 317 days and remain in or near the nest for some 14 days before dispersing.

ABUNDANCE: Common

DIET: Invertebrates, fish, frogs, lizards, snakes, mammals, birds and their eggs, and carrion

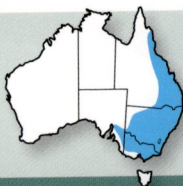

SIZE: Average total length 1.5 m, maximum length 2 m

STATUS: Secure

Opposite: Some Lace Monitors, particularly from dry regions, are handsomely marked with broad black and yellow crossbands. A single clutch of eggs may produce both broad-banded and normally patterned hatchlings. **Above:** Lace Monitors are excellent climbers, scaling tall trees with ease.

Skinks

Family: Scincidae

Skinks are diverse and abundant in Australia, ranging from Tasmania to the Torres Strait Islands and from Queensland's rainforest to Western Australia's Great Sandy Desert. About 380 species are recorded and new skinks are regularly being discovered and named.

Most skinks are active during the day, but others forage at night or during late afternoon and early morning. Some skinks move about either during the day or at night — depending on the prevailing temperature.

A typical skink is agile and quick. It is small to medium-sized, with a slender, streamlined body and shiny overlapping scales that are tight fitting and firm to the touch. The tapering tail is longer than its body and the limbs each have five toes and claws. It has moveable eyelids and visible ear openings. But some skinks don't fit this general description and there is indeed much variation within the family.

Some small skinks lead a hidden lifestyle, burrowing in loose soil, sand or leaf litter. Many of these burrowing skinks have long slender bodies and degenerate limbs, or have no limbs at all.

Most skinks live on the ground and shelter in a burrow. A skink's burrow is often situated beneath a rock or log, or the entrance is hidden within low vegetation. Some skinks inhabit outcropping rock and hide in a narrow crevice. Tree dwelling skinks hide under loose bark or in a hollow.

Many skinks readily sacrifice their fragile tails when seized by a predator. In time, a new tail sprouts from the stump of the original.

Small skinks feed primarily on insects. Larger skinks also eat insects as well as worms, snails, small lizards, fruit, flowers and fungi.

A majority of skinks lay eggs, but the skink family also includes the only Australian lizards to bear their young alive.

Top: The Major Skink (*Egernia frerei*) inhabits rainforest and other humid environments along the east coast of Queensland. It basks in patches of sunlight on the forest floor.

Top: As its name suggests, the Limbless Snake-toothed Skink (*Coeranoscincus frontalis*) has no external trace of limbs. This secretive skink burrows in loose soil beneath logs and leaf litter in rainforests. It occurs in the Atherton Tableland district of north-eastern Queensland. **Above:** The Ocellated Skink (*Niveoscincus ocellatus*) is confined to Tasmania and the Bass Strait Islands. This cold-tolerant skink survives in areas where it snows annually. It emerges from a rock crevice to bask in a sheltered position, even on cold, windy days.

The seasonal colour change of male rainbow skinks is unknown among other skinks. Presumably males develop their bright pattern to advertise their presence to rival males or to attract the attention of females. Both male and female rainbow skinks further draw attention to themselves by lifting and wriggling their tail in the air. Why they do this is not understood, but the activity is most intense during social interaction, when two skinks approach each other in leaf litter.

DESCRIPTION: Rainbow Skinks are small, moderate to robust skinks with a medium length, slender tail. The body of this crevice-dwelling species is flattened from above. The scales on the back are either smooth, or with two or three weak to strong keels. The forelimbs have four toes and the hindlimbs five. With the exception of one species, the Tree Base Litter Skink (*Carlia foliorum*), which has a fixed scale covering the eye, all have a moveable lower eyelid enclosing a transparent disc. Rainbow skinks are so named because of the iridescent sheen of their scales and the colourful patterns displayed by breeding males. The spectacular male breeding colours vary between species and might include metallic blue-green on the head and bright orange or red stripes on the sides. Females and immature males are more sombre brownish in colour.

HABITAT: Most rainbow skinks occur in woodland or dry sclerophyll forest. A few extend into dry shrubland and grassland and two species live in wet sclerophyll forest and rainforest.

BEHAVIOUR: The sun-loving rainbow skinks have a preference for areas with an abundant covering of leaf litter. They shelter beneath fallen timber or rocks. Some species inhabit rock outcrops and live in a tight crevice.

BREEDING: Female rainbow skinks lay two eggs per clutch.

Jewel Rainbow Skink   *Carlia jarnoldae*

ABUNDANCE: Common
DIET: Small invertebrates
SIZE: Average total length 10 cm
STATUS: Secure

Left: Male (background) and female (foreground) Jewel Rainbow Skinks.

Closed Litter Rainbow Skink

Carlia longipes

ABUNDANCE: Common
DIET: Small invertebrates
SIZE: Average total length 15 cm
STATUS: Secure

Shaded Litter Rainbow Skink

Carlia munda

ABUNDANCE: Common
DIET: Small invertebrates
SIZE: Average total length 10 cm
STATUS: Secure

Blue-lipped Rainbow Skink

Carlia rhomboidalis

ABUNDANCE: Common
DIET: Small invertebrates
SIZE: Average total length 13 cm
STATUS: Secure

Swanson's Snake-eyed Skink is confined to the northern coast of the Northern Territory. It is common in suburban Darwin, where it is usually seen climbing on fences or on the walls of buildings. This enterprising lizard is known to rob ant columns of their load of larvae and insects.

DESCRIPTION: This arboreal Snake-eyed Skink has a slender body that is markedly flattened from above. Its slender tail is medium length and the limbs are relatively long. The scales are smooth and the large eye is covered with a fixed transparent disc. The colour of the back and sides is pale grey to greyish-brown with numerous black flecks. There is a ragged silvery-grey stripe on the outer edges of the back extending from above the eye onto the tail. The head often has a coppery flush. The undersurface is white.

HABITAT: This common skink is an inhabitant of woodlands and dry sclerophyll forest.

BEHAVIOUR: Swanson's Snake-eyed Skink lives in trees, occasionally among rocks, and commonly on buildings and other built structures in cities and towns. It is an adept climber that makes short jumps between branches while manoeuvring in the treetops. Typically it rests in a sunny position low down on a tree trunk and quickly climbs the tree when approached. At night it shelters beneath loose bark or in folds and crevices of standing and fallen trees.

BREEDING: Females lay two eggs per clutch.

ABUNDANCE: Very common
DIET: Small invertebrates

SIZE: Average total length 10 cm
STATUS: Secure

The Pink-tongued Skink climbs trees effortlessly using its strong claws and prehensile tail. It is occasionally encountered in well-established suburban gardens.

DESCRIPTION: The Pink-tongued Skink has a long and moderately robust body. The head is large and also long. The tail is long, slender and somewhat prehensile. The limbs have long toes with sharp recurved claws. Its scales are smooth and glossy. The colour of the back and sides is more or less uniform pale grey to brown-grey or pinkish-grey with a blackish tip on the snout. There are usually prominent to obscure dark brown to black crossbands on the body and tail. The tongue of an adult is pink in colour, that of a juvenile is dark blue. Juveniles have clearly defined and strongly contrasting bands. The undersurface is brownish in colour.

HABITAT: The Pink-tongued Skink lives in humid woodland, sclerophyll forests and rainforest.

BEHAVIOUR: The Pink-tongued Skink is at home both in trees or on the ground. It is most active at sundown or during the hours of darkness, but it is occasionally seen basking at the entrance of its shelter site. It lives in hollows of standing and fallen trees, in rock crevices or beneath rocks and timber lying on the ground.

BREEDING: A female Pink-tongued Skink gives birth to a large number of small live young. The average litter size is about fifteen, but as many as 33 have been recorded.

Above: The strongly contrasting pattern of a juvenile Pink-tongued Skink becomes obscure with age.

ABUNDANCE: Uncommon

DIET: Primarily snails and slugs, also insects

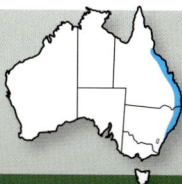

SIZE: Average total length 40 cm

STATUS: Secure

Striped skinks   *Ctenotus* spp.

With about 95 members, the striped skinks are the largest genus of Australian lizards. In arid Australia, where they reach the greatest abundance, as many as six species may share the same habitat. They are able to coexist because of subtle differences in the prey preference or activity period of each species.

DESCRIPTION: Striped skinks are typical skinks, small to medium-sized, slender to moderately robust and with a medium length, slender tail. The scales are smooth and glossy. The limbs are well developed and each has five toes. The lower eyelid is moveable. Most striped skinks have a pattern on the back and sides consisting of lengthwise stripes extending the full length of the body and most of the tail or, more usually, a combination of stripes and spots. Many species are superficially similar and often difficult to identify, particularly from a brief glimpse of a swiftly moving skink in bushland.

HABITAT: The majority of striped skinks occur in dry shrubland and grassland or dry woodland. Many inhabit humid woodland in northern Australia and a few occur in the sclerophyll forests of eastern and south-western Australia.

BEHAVIOUR: Striped skinks are swift-moving, sun-loving skinks. In arid regions they regulate their body temperature during the day by moving between sunlit and shaded areas. At night, or in cold weather, they shelter in a burrow, often at the base of a low shrub or grass hummock, or beneath rock and fallen timber. Striped skinks are ground-dwelling lizards, but occasionally climb about in grass hummocks or low shrubs. Some striped skinks are active at very high temperatures in the middle of the day.

BREEDING: Most striped skinks lay two or three eggs but some large species may produce up to nine eggs per clutch.

Leopard Skink   *Ctenotus pantherinus*

ABUNDANCE: Common
DIET: Small invertebrates
SIZE: Average total length 25 cm
STATUS: Secure

Pretty Striped Skink
Ctenotus pulchellus

ABUNDANCE: Common
DIET: Small invertebrates
SIZE: Average total length 18 cm
STATUS: Secure

Robust Striped Skink
Ctenotus robustus

ABUNDANCE: Very common
DIET: Small invertebrates
SIZE: Average total length 30 cm
STATUS: Secure

Schomburgk's Striped Skink
Ctenotus schomburgkii

ABUNDANCE: Common
DIET: Small invertebrates
SIZE: Average total length 15 cm
STATUS: Secure

The Depressed Spiny Skink inflates its body and uses its spiny tail to wedge itself tightly into a crevice.

DESCRIPTION: The Depressed Spiny Skink has a robust body, somewhat flattened from above. The tail is very short, broad and also flattened. The scales of the back and sides each have three spiny keels and these are larger and more spiny on the tail. The Depressed Spiny Skink varies geographically. In northern populations the colour of the back and sides is reddish-brown with an obscure darker crosswise pattern and scattered blackish spots on the rear of the body and tail. Southern populations are reddish-brown to yellowish-brown on the forebody becoming pale grey on the rear of the body and with blackish-brown spots that may form an irregular crosswise pattern. The undersurface is cream.

HABITAT: The Depressed Spiny Skink inhabits dry shrubland and grassland or dry woodland, often where there is outcropping rock.

BEHAVIOUR: This skink is a shy lizard which basks at the entrance of its shelter site and silently retreats when approached. In the north of its range it lives in rock outcrops and shelters in crevices or beneath exfoliating slabs of rock. It also dwells in the cavities of large termite mounds. Southern populations are mainly arboreal, living in hollows and cracks of standing or fallen trees.

BREEDING: A female gives birth to two live young per litter.

ABUNDANCE: Common
DIET: Small invertebrates

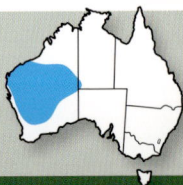

SIZE: Average total length 14 cm
STATUS: Secure

The Land Mullet is a conspicuous and powerful lizard and Australia's largest skink. It gets its common name from its shiny fish-like scales.

DESCRIPTION: The Land Mullet is a moderately robust skink. The tail is medium length and slender, but somewhat thickened at the base. Its scales are glossy with multiple weak keels. The colour of the back and sides is uniform black-brown to black. Juveniles have small bluish-white spots on the sides. The undersurface is white, yellow or orange.

HABITAT: The Land Mullet is an inhabitant of rainforest and wet sclerophyll forest. It is confined to cool higher altitude forest in the northern parts of its range. It usually occurs on the edge of the forest, near tracks, or where a large tree has fallen to provide a break in the canopy.

BEHAVIOUR: The Land Mullet lives in the hollow of a decaying log or in a burrow beneath a fallen tree, usually close to dense vegetation. It basks in patches of sunlight and retreats noisily to its shelter when approached. Small social groups of Land Mullets, including adults, subadults and juveniles, often occupy the same shelter site. Large adults are very tolerant of the juveniles.

BREEDING: A female Land Mullet gives birth to 4–9 live young per litter.

Above: Juvenile Land Mullet.

ABUNDANCE: Uncommon
DIET: Insects, worms, snails, slugs, fallen fruit and fungi

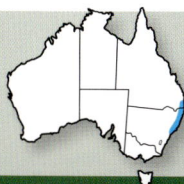

SIZE: Average total length 50 cm, maximum length 70 cm
STATUS: Secure

When pursued, the Narrow-banded Sand Swimmer pushes into loose sand and "swims" beneath the surface to escape. It also erupts from a partly submerged position in loose sand to seize passing prey.

DESCRIPTION: The Narrow-banded Sand Swimmer has a mid-sized body and a medium length, slender tail. Its snout is pointed, and its scales are glossy, and smooth to weakly keeled. These features facilitate "swimming" through sand. The back and sides are pale yellow to golden brown with narrow brownish crossbands. The bands range 10–19 on the body and 35–40 on the tail. This pattern may be prominent to obscure and some may be very pale with no indication of a pattern. The bands are more or less uniform, but sometimes irregular and branching. The undersurface is white.

HABITAT: Sandy areas with an abundance of spinifex grass are particularly important habitat, with dry shrubland and grassland or dry woodland vegetation.

BEHAVIOUR: This is a nocturnal skink. During the day it remains concealed in loose sand beneath leaf litter, under fallen timber or in a burrow. At night it emerges to forage widely on sandy plains and dunes. The Narrow-banded Sand Swimmer has an aggressive temperament and will not tolerate other lizards — including members of its own species — at close quarters.

BREEDING: This species is an egg-layer, and a female lays from 2–5 eggs per clutch.

ABUNDANCE: Uncommon
DIET: Invertebrates and small lizards, particularly of the genus *Lerista*

SIZE: Average total length 20 cm
STATUS: Secure

The semi-aquatic Golden Water Skink is found by water and in cooler microclimates. It will readily enter the water and swim to the opposite bank to escape a predator, or it may dive and remain submerged for up to 30 minutes. Its slightly flattened tail provides extra thrust for swimming.

DESCRIPTION: The Golden Water Skink has a moderately robust body with a deep head. The tail is medium length, slender and slightly flattened at the sides. Its scales are smooth and glossy. The back and sides are yellowish to olive-brown usually with scattered black flecks. A narrow golden-yellow stripe extends from above the eye along the outer edge of the neck to the forebody. A broad black zone on the upper sides encloses small cream spots. The lower sides are cream with blackish variegation or spots. The sides of the tail have numerous black flecks and the limbs are yellowish-brown with black spots. Underparts are white to yellowish, often with lengthwise grey lines on the throat and chest.

HABITAT: The Golden Water Skink occurs along waterways in humid woodlands, sclerophyll forests and rainforest. It also inhabits stormwater drains in built-up areas of large cities.

BEHAVIOUR: The Golden Water Skink shelters in a burrow beneath a rock or log usually at the edge of permanent water. In the morning it emerges from its burrow to bask and, once warmed, forages on the bank for insects or in the water for tadpoles and frogs.

BREEDING: A female produces from 2–10 live young per litter.

ABUNDANCE: Common
DIET: Invertebrates, fish, tadpoles, frogs, small lizards and berries

SIZE: Average total length 25 cm
STATUS: Secure

The Delicate Skink is more common in suburban gardens than in adjacent native bushland.

DESCRIPTION: The Delicate Skink has a moderate body with a medium length, slender tail. Its scales are smooth. The back and sides are greyish-brown to rich brown, often with darker and paler flecks. A narrow yellowish-brown stripe is usually present on the outer edge of the back. There is a broad black stripe on the upper sides, sometimes with a thin whitish line below. The lower sides are greyish brown with lighter and darker peppering. The top of the head and nape are usually coppery brown and the tail often has a bluish flush. The undersurface is white or cream in colour.

HABITAT: This common skink occurs in open heath, humid woodland, sclerophyll forests and on the fringe of rainforest. It appears to prefer very open, loose leaf litter — perhaps to maximise exposure to warm sunlight as it hunts for food. It is also abundant on farmland.

BEHAVIOUR: The Delicate Skink basks on low lying timber or rocks and disappears into leaf litter or beneath debris when approached. At night it shelters under rocks, fallen timber or urban debris such as sheet iron.

BREEDING: A female Delicate Skink lays from 1–8 eggs per clutch and the eggs measure about 7.5 mm long by 5 mm wide. Communal nesting sites are often encountered in moist soil beneath garden debris and may contain up to 250 eggs. Why many skinks choose the same nesting site when there are apparently many equally suitable sites nearby is a mystery.

Above: A communal nesting site of the Delicate Skink.

ABUNDANCE: Very common
DIET: Small invertebrates

SIZE: Average total length 10 cm
STATUS: Secure

With its very small limbs, the South-eastern Slider can choose how it moves. On a firm surface it uses the limbs, but in loose soil or leaf litter, the limbs are held against the body, and the skink undulates, leaving wavy patterns in the sand. Perhaps the most interesting feature of the genus Lerista *is the wide variation in the degree of limb reduction among the species.*

DESCRIPTION: This species has a long body with a medium length tail slightly narrower than the body. Its scales are smooth and glossy. Both forelimbs and hindlimbs have five toes. The lower eyelid is moveable and a small ear opening is present. The back and sides are grey to brown, sometimes with small, dark spots aligned lengthwise. A broad blackish stripe on the upper sides extends from the snout to the base of the tail. The lower sides are cream, sometimes with darker streaks. The tail is usually brown or orange with small dark spots. Underparts are white or cream.

HABITAT: Heath, dry sclerophyll forest and woodland are preferred, where an open canopy allows sunlight through to warm leaf litter and soil.

BEHAVIOUR: This skink shelters beneath rocks or fallen timber resting on loose soil. When disturbed it pushes into the soil to escape. It rarely ventures to the surface and, if it does, only at night.

BREEDING: Across its range, the species has a variable mode of reproduction. Mainland populations lay 2–4 eggs, while those from Tasmania, the Bass Strait Islands and Kangaroo Island produce 2–4 live young. Populations from the south coast of Victoria are intermediate, laying eggs which hatch after a short incubation period of about 19 days.

ABUNDANCE: Common
DIET: Small, soft-bodied invertebrates

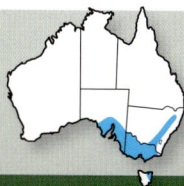

SIZE: Average total length 12 cm
STATUS: Secure

The Pygmy Blue-tongue appears to have disappeared from much of its former range, probably due to land clearing. It was not sighted for 33 years and thought to be extinct. In 1992 it was rediscovered near Burra, South Australia, by a herpetologist who found a recently swallowed specimen inside a road-killed Eastern Brown Snake (Pseudonaja textilis).

DESCRIPTION: The Pygmy Blue-tongue has a robust body, large head and short limbs. The moderately short slender tail is slightly flattened at the sides. Its scales are smooth. The back and sides are variable: either uniform yellowish-brown to greyish-brown or with a scattering of blackish-brown streaks and blotches. Its undersurface is cream or bluish-white.

HABITAT: Originally Pygmy Blue-tongues were collected from mallee scrublands, where they sheltered in hollows of mallee roots or beneath limestone slabs. Existing populations inhabit rolling, treeless grassland plains and live in spider holes.

BEHAVIOUR: The Pygmy Blue-tongue lives in a tight-fitting vertical spider burrow. During the day it sits at the top of its burrow and ambushes passing prey. It shelters at the base of the burrow at night.

BREEDING: A female Pygmy Blue-tongue produces from 1–4 live young and they live in their mother's burrow for about 12 weeks before dispersing. The male reportedly drags the female from its burrow by the head to mate.

ABUNDANCE: Rare
DIET: Insects, spiders, snails, small lizards and fruit

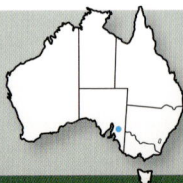

SIZE: Average total length 15 cm
STATUS: Endangered

The Centralian Blue-tongue opens its mouth widely, hisses loudly and protrudes its cobalt-blue tongue in warning when threatened. It inflates its body in an effort to appear larger than it is, tucks its small legs in close and angles its broadest aspect towards its tormentor.

DESCRIPTION: The Centralian Blue-tongue has a short, robust body, large broad head, short limbs and a moderately short tail. Its scales are smooth. The colour of the back and sides is yellow, fawn or pale greyish with somewhat irregular reddish-brown or orange bands. These bands are often strongly contrasting. A very prominent black streak extends from behind the eye to the back of the head. There may be black in the grooves between some of the head shields. The side of the neck has a blackish smudge and the outer surfaces of the limbs are usually blackish. The undersurface is white to cream.

HABITAT: The Centralian Blue-tongue inhabits dry shrubland and grassland or dry woodland particularly where there is an abundance of spinifex grass. It occurs on sandy plains and dunes, also in rocky areas.

BEHAVIOUR: The Centralian Blue-tongue is active during early morning, late afternoon and on warm nights. It shelters in a burrow or within a dense spinifex grass hummock.

BREEDING: A female Centralian Blue-tongue produces 2–7 live young.

ABUNDANCE: Common
DIET: Invertebrates and fruit

SIZE: Average total length 30 cm
STATUS: Secure

The cold-tolerant Blotched Blue-tongue is the only large lizard inhabiting Tasmania. In the north of its range in New South Wales it is restricted to cool elevated slopes of the Great Dividing Range.

DESCRIPTION: The Blotched Blue-tongue has a robust body, large broad head, short limbs and a moderately short tail. Its scales are smooth. Colour and pattern vary geographically. The southern lowland form is dark brown to blackish above, with large greyish, fawn or pale pink blotches, more or less in a lengthwise alignment. The sides are greyish or fawn with irregular dark brown bars or variegation. The New South Wales alpine form is larger and more robust than the southern form. It is black with large yellow, orange or pink blotches, in a lengthwise alignment. The sides are yellow with black lengthwise streaks or variegation. The blotches usually join to form cross-bands on the tail. The undersurface is white to yellow with dark variegation.

HABITAT: The Blotched Blue-tongue occurs in alpine grassland, heath, humid woodland and sclerophyll forests. It spends winter in deep, warm leaf litter, hollow logs or rock crevices.

BEHAVIOUR: This species is active during the day and shelters at night in a hollow log or in a burrow beneath rock.

BREEDING: A male Blotched Blue-tongue intent on mating chases the female and grips the side of her body firmly in his jaws in the area behind her front legs. He maintains his grip for the duration of copulation. A female usually produces about six live young, but litters of up to fifteen are recorded. The young often remain together for a number of days following birth.

ABUNDANCE: Common
DIET: Insects, slugs, snails, seeds and fruit

SIZE: Average total length 45 cm
STATUS: Secure

Shingleback *Tiliqua rugosa*

The Shingleback is an abundant and familiar lizard in much of southern Australia. It is known by a variety of common names including Sleepy Lizard, Stump-tailed Lizard and Pine Cone Lizard.

DESCRIPTION: The Shingleback has a short, very robust body and a large, broad, triangular head. The tail is very short and swollen. The scales on the back are large and rough, resembling a pine cone in appearance. Its colour and pattern are highly variable. The colour of the back and sides is uniform blackish-brown, reddish-brown to yellowish brown, or with a few to many yellow, cream or whitish spots. The spots occasionally dominate or form irregular crosswise bands. South-western populations usually have a yellow or orange flush on the head. The undersurface is variable. It is sometimes similar to the colour above, or whitish with dark streaks or bars.

HABITAT: The Shingleback inhabits dry shrubland and grassland, dry woodland, dry sclerophyll forest and heath.

BEHAVIOUR: This ponderous lizard shelters under low shrubs, beneath fallen timber, in a hollow log, or in the burrows of rabbits and wombats. It emerges in the morning to forage nearby for plant matter. When disturbed a Shingleback's first reaction is to lay motionless against the ground. If harassed it gapes its mouth widely and extends its dark blue tongue in warning.

BREEDING: Male and female Shinglebacks form long-term bonds. Each year in the breeding season, pairs are known to seek out their partners of previous seasons. This pairing association may continue over a ten year period. A female Shingleback gives birth to between one and four (usually two) relatively large, live young.

ABUNDANCE: Common
DIET: Mainly fruit, flowers and other plant matter, also fungi, snails, insects, carrion and mammal droppings

SIZE: Average total length 35 cm
STATUS: Secure

Glossary

AGAMID A member of the family Agamidae, the "dragons".

ARBOREAL Tree-dwelling.

DIURNAL Active during the day.

DORSAL Describing the upper surface, or back.

GULAR Pertaining to the throat.

HERPETOCULTURE The keeping of reptiles as pets.

HERPETOLOGIST A person who studies reptiles.

KEEL A raised lengthwise ridge, either on the body or on individual scales.

MICROHABITAT A small area of habitat.

NOCTURNAL Active at night.

NUCHAL Pertaining to the back of the neck.

PARTHENOGENETIC Able to reproduce without male fertilisation.

SCLEROPHYLL FOREST Eucalypt-dominated forest.

TERRARIUM An enclosure for keeping small reptiles.

TERRESTRIAL Ground-dwelling.

TUBERCLE A small nodule or protrusion.

VARIEGATED Having varied or different colours.

VENTRAL Describing the lower surface, or stomach.

VERTEBRAL Mid-line of back.

Index

Links & Further Reading

Books

Cogger, H. G. *Reptiles & Amphibians of Australia,* 6th Edition, Reed New Holland, Sydney, 2000

Ehmann, H. *Encyclopedia of Australian Animals: Reptiles,* Collins Angus & Robertson, Sydney, 1992

Greer, A. E. *The Biology and Evolution of Australian Lizards,* Surrey Beatty & Sons, Sydney, 1989

Horner, P. *Skinks of the Northern Territory,* Northern Territory Museum of Arts and Sciences, Darwin, 1992

Houston, T. and Hutchinson, M. *Dragon Lizards and Goannas of South Australia,* South Australia Museum, Adelaide, 1998

Hutchinson, M., Swain, R. and Driessen, M. *Snakes and Lizards of Tasmania,* University of Tasmania, Hobart, 2001

Storr, G. M., Smith, L. A. and Johnstone, R. E. *Lizards of Western Australia I: Skinks,* Western Australian Museum, Perth, 1999

Storr, G. M., Smith, L. A. and Johnstone, R. E. *Lizards of Western Australia II: Dragons and Monitors,* Western Australian Museum, Perth, 1983

Storr, G. M., Smith, L. A. and Johnstone, R. E. *Lizards of Western Australia III: Geckos & Pygopods,* Western Australian Museum, Perth, 1990

Swan, G., Shea, G. and Sadlier, R. *A Field Guide to Reptiles of New South Wales,* New Holland Publishers Pty. Ltd., Australia, 2004

Swanson, S. *Amazing Facts about Australian Reptiles,* Steve Parish Publishing Pty. Ltd., Brisbane, 2008

Swanson, S. *Field Guide to Australian Reptiles,* Steve Parish Publishing Pty. Ltd., Brisbane, 2007

Weigel, J. *Care of Australian Reptiles in Captivity,* Reptile Keepers Association, 1998

Wilson, S. *A Field Guide to Reptiles of Queensland,* New Holland Publishers Pty. Ltd., Australia, 2005

Wilson, S. and Swan, G. *A Complete Guide to Reptiles of Australia,* New Holland Publishers Pty. Ltd., Australia, 2003

Websites

Aussie Reptile Keeper
www.aussiereptilekeeper.com

Australian Herpetological Society
www.ahs.org.au

Australian Museum (Herpetology)
www.amonline.net.au/herpetology

Reptiles Australia Magazine
www.reptilesaustralia.com.au

The Reptiles of Australia
www.kingsnake.com/oz

Published by Steve Parish Publishing Pty Ltd
PO Box 1058, Archerfield, Qld 4108 Australia

www.steveparish.com.au

ISBN 978174193409 0

First published 2008

Principal photography: Stephen Swanson

Additional photography: Steve Parish: pp. 1-2, 9
(centre left), 10, 12-13, 24, 42, 43 (top), 50, 55, 57
(bottom), 59, 69, 73, 89 & 91; Michael Cermak:
p. 6; Ian Morris: pp. 7, 14, 39 (top), 57 (top) & 67
(top); Gary Steer: p. 11 (bottom); Ken Stepnell/
SPP: pp. 9 (top right), 49, 51 (top) & 90

Front cover image: Frilled Lizard, Darwin, NT.

Title page image: Eastern Water Dragon,
Steve Parish.
Inset: Lace Monitor (above) & Western Hooded
Scaly-foot (below), Steve Parish.

Text: Stephen Swanson
Design: Leanne Nobilio, SPP
Editorial: Grant McDuling; Helen Anderson &
Sarah Lowe, SPP
Production: Tina Brewster, SPP

Prepress by Colour Chiefs Digital Imaging,
Brisbane, Australia
Printed in Singapore by Imago

**Produced in Australia at the Steve Parish
Publishing Studios**